To Marilyn
I hope you enjoy this
true history of my
father. Enjoy.

Kris Clark
9/5/11

$50 IN MY POCKET

I'm off to see America

An Historical Memoir

by

Lis Clark

authorHOUSE®

AuthorHouse™
1663 Liberty Drive
Bloomington, IN 47403
www.authorhouse.com
Phone: 1-800-839-8640

©2010 Lis Clark. All rights reserved.

No part of this book may be reproduced, stored in a retrieval system, or transmitted by any means without the written permission of the author.

First published by AuthorHouse 1/25/2010

ISBN: 978-1-4490-5663-6 (e)
ISBN: 978-1-4490-5665-0 (sc)
ISBN: 978-1-4490-5664-3 (hc)

Library of Congress Control Number: 2009912998

Printed in the United States of America
Bloomington, Indiana

This book is printed on acid-free paper.

DEDICATION

This book is dedicated to all the immigrants who passed through Ellis Island with $50.00 in their pockets ready to start a new life in this new land. They are the people who worked from sunup to sundown, for very little pay. They opened new frontiers to make a better life for themselves and their families and made a major contribution towards making this country the greatest country in the world. Let us hope that the generations who have followed will realize that freedom takes hard work and vigilance to maintain this countries greatness.

A special dedication to Haldor's grandchildren Deborah Waarkjaer, David and Erik Helleskov

CHAPTERS

CHAPTER ONE — 1
The Trip at Sea

CHAPTER TWO — 9
Arrival at New York with $50.00 in My Pocket

CHAPTER THREE — 17
Finding A Job

CHAPTER FOUR — 29
A New Job

CHAPTER FIVE — 49
Finally, I Got the New Car

CHAPTER SIX — 65
Off to Bermuda

CHAPTER SEVEN — 101
We Say Goodby To Bermuda

CHAPTER EIGHT — 119
Meeting "Teddy"

CHAPTER NINE — 135
The Trip South

CHAPTER TEN — 167
Back Home To Chatham

CHAPTER ELEVEN — 191
New Job In Connecticut

CHAPTER TWELVE — 201
Tragedy Strikes

PREFACE

These letters were translated verbatim, including incorrect grammar. Remember, as you read the text, that Haldor had limited knowledge of English and learned to speak the language by imitating the spoken words around him and those are the words he used to describe what he was experiencing.

Some of the language used in his letters is not politically correct in today's society but in no way was it meant to be condescending. I grappled with the decision to change the wording to be politically correct but in the end, I chose not to change the text. This was the normal language of the people that he associated with. I wanted this to be a true reflection of Haldor's experiences, travels and his interaction with the people he met along the way.

We have always been a land with many immigrants speaking all manner of languages. I hope, as you read these letters, you will realize how difficult it was for Haldor to assimilate himself into an unfamiliar society.

Enjoy reading this historical account of one man's adventure and I hope that it gives you, the reader, the courage to follow your dreams and adventures.

Respectfully,

Lis Clark

Marie and Lauritz Baarvig
Haldor's mother and father to whom the letters are written

Haldor on Dock waiting to board ship

S/S UNITED STATES

CHAPTER ONE

The Trip at Sea

S/S United States
Friday June 2. 1916

Dear Mom and Dad,

We left Copenhagen Thursday, June 1st, on the ship S/S UNITED STATES. The trip to Kristiania[1], Norway was good. The wind was strong, but I was not seasick and had a nice cabin with three other young men. I had a lower berth and slept well. This morning June 2nd, we were docked in Kristiania. The next stop will be Kristianssand on the lower coast of Norway then to Kirkwall, Scotland. We left Kristiania

---

1 Now called Oslo

this afternoon at 4 o'clock. The wind had increased and big waves were running up Kristiania Fjord. I stayed on the top deck so I wouldn't get seasick, but as we rounded the South Coast of Norway and headed west toward the North Sea, the ship started rolling from side to side. It takes ten hours of sailing to get to Kristianssand and by 6 p.m. dinner time, not many showed up to eat. Big waves splashed over the lower decks, and I felt sick. I kept going until 10 o'clock, when I finally went down and managed to get to bed. I found I felt better in bed with my head low and on my back, and stayed like that until I fell asleep.

Saturday June 3

At 3 o'clock in the morning we pulled into Kristianssand and it was nice to have a deck under your feet that didn't heave and tip and jump. We were not allowed off the ship and we left again at 4 o'clock in a storm that sent huge waves up the harbor. We were now in the North Sea, and I tried to stay up, but I started to throw up and had to lean over the railing - I was far from being the only one to do that - so it was back to bed. The old ship was dancing and jumping and shaking. I stayed here and I felt fairly good when in bed, but if I tried to get up I would get nauseated again. We got to Kirkwall, Scotland, Sunday morning at 6 o'clock, and left again in the evening, so I had a chance to eat something that day and keep it down.

Monday June 5.
Morning

We are now in the Atlantic Ocean. One hour after leaving Kirkwall last night in the storm, I started to throw up and it was back to bed for me - I feel fairly good when I stay there. My clothes hanging on the wall are swinging out when the ship rolls at a 25 degree angle, and I keep watching them to make sure they don't jump off the hook. I am writing this in bed and I know it will be four or six weeks before you will get it.I don't feel so well now, but I have to try to get on the deck today.

Monday 6:30 p.m.

We are now a good bit out in the Atlantic, and I have been thinking of the saying that the North Sea is more choppy than the Atlantic, and makes people seasick much faster and worse than the Atlantic - I know I feel better, not much appetite yet and I have a headache, but I can begin to talk to people and notice what is going on. There are people of all nationalities - Danes, Germans, English, Americans, Swedish, Norwegians, Finns, Russians, Polish, Armenians, Turks, Spanish, Italians and Persians, and you hear all these languages spoken. We all try to talk to one another and usually can make out all right. I am eating my meals at a table with three Finnish people - two young girls and a young man - I talk to them and already know some Finnish. They are nice clean and well-dressed people like the Danes, and they tell me there are two kinds of people in Finland. The Finnish Eskimos in the North and the other Finnish people in the city are mostly of Swedish descent.

We have one hour of music every afternoon from 4 p.m.. to 5 p.m.. The ship's orchestra plays special string music sometimes, and sometimes dance music. Sometimes it is on the deck, and this afternoon people were dancing and a big wave hit the ship and splashed over the deck - everybody got soaked.

Tuesday, June 6

One week from today we should be in New York if we make it in 11 days. It is not easy to believe that we are moving. We see water and water and more water, and it looks to be the same every day. This ship is the center and nothing changes. Even the seagulls flying around the ship seem to be the same ones we saw yesterday. We are now about 800 miles from the nearest land - we are moving about 300 miles every day and night (23 hours and 33 minutes) and I am told that it is about 3500 miles from Copenhagen to New York. There is six hours difference in the time, except now that you have advanced your clocks one hour there will be seven hours difference. The weather is better and it should be warmer as we are going farther South as well as West. New York is about the same parallel as Lisbon and Madrid or Napoli.

Today we saw a dolphin jumping and following the ship. It looked to be about four to six yards long and it easily followed, jumping entirely out of the water every few seconds.

Wednesday June 7, 10 p.m.

It's a nice day, still on the cold side, no wind, and we can feel we are farther South. Today we saw three sharks - they were big and ugly looking. They are looking for garbage thrown from the ship. We are hoping for weather like this 'til we get to New York.

Thursday June 8, 10 p.m.

One week ago we left Copenhagen and today we entered the Gulf Stream. We will follow that for a while. Now the air is warmer and the water is a warm 65 degrees. The daylight is getting shorter and we are getting farther South, and it is now dark by 9 p.m.. We miss having daylight in Denmark until 11p.m., with the sun up at 1 a.m.. Today we saw a whole colony of sharks following the ship, and the seagulls are still with us. We hope to get to New York by Tuesday next week.

Friday June 9

Yesterday's good weather is no more. Today it is blowing up to a storm, but now I am getting used to the sea, and the ship's pitching doesn't bother me too much. Some people here are seasick, The waves are getting real bad and break over the deck, so no one is allowed on deck. We are locked in. I am sitting here on this chair holding on with one hand and writing with the other to keep from sliding all over the place. I am glad I am not sick and I hope to stay that way. We are now on a parallel with Paris.

Saturday June 10

The storm didn't last long - it is much better today, but last night it was rough. After I got to bed, a big wave hit the ship and everything on the stand by my bed fell over on my head, but today it is nice on deck, the ship is fairly steady.

We passed an iceberg floating in the Atlantic about in the spot that the Titanic went down; luckily it was daylight and we could see it for a long distance. The ship changed course to go closer and when we passed it, it was 400 to 800 yards away. It was beautiful, shining like a marble in the sun. It was higher than the ship and as only 1/10 of it is above water, it was a big iceberg. It must have been frozen snow, white and clean. I am glad we didn't hit it.

I am sorry to see the sun go down so early now - about 8 p.m. - and it gets real dark at night except for the moon. Tonight the moon is bright and I was standing on the aft deck by the railing and the wake of the ship made a silver river flowing away from us. It is completely calm weather, and I was thinking of you and Denmark so far away. Now it is toward morning there and you are all in bed and asleep. How is your weather? Where at night, it is light enough to read a newspaper outside at midnight. That is the North and it is known for that. And that I must do without now. It is something you miss and think about when you don't have it anymore. Now, near the end of my ocean trip I miss you all, and now when the serious part soon will begin, I think of Denmark. I hope Mr. Moldenhaver has a job for me as he promised. I have 50 dollars in my pocket. That is a must when you land on Ellis Island. That should last me for some time.

Saturday June 10

Tomorrow is a holiday in Denmark (Pinse) and as usual also the day after 2nd Pinseday. Here is one day like other days, and you lose track of the time. I wonder where all the seagulls come from, there seem to

Lis Clark

be 1000's of them following the ship. Are they the same ones we saw in the North Sea? Now off to bed.

Monday June 12

I am still thinking about you and Denmark. Today is a holiday as was yesterday (Sunday). We had some fog last night for about one hour, and you could hear the engines slow down. We were barely moving and every few seconds the whistle blew. It was not very nice to hear - some people were afraid and dressed and went up on deck. If we don't get slowed down by more fog, we will be in New York tomorrow or tonight after 12 midnight. What is ahead? I don't know. Time will tell, but I'm looking forward to whatever it is.

Ship's Manifest Page 1 (see last line #30)

$50 In My Pocket

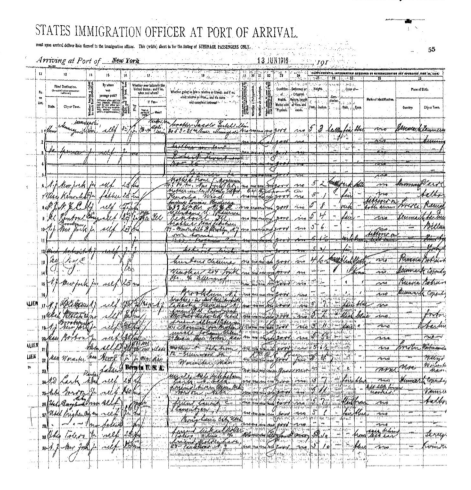

Ship's Manifest Page 2 (see last line #30)

CHAPTER TWO

Arrival at New York with $50.00 in My Pocket

Tuesday June 13

It is wonderful and unbelievably beautiful here. We are stopped at the entrance to New York Bay, with Long Island on one side and New Jersey on the other side. It is 6 a.m. in the morning and the sky is clear and the air is warm. We are waiting for the Customs and Immigration officials, then we will proceed up the Bay while we eat breakfast. We can't see New York yet, but soon we will be there at Ellis Island and we have to go through the tough entrance to the New World. I can see beautiful estates along the shores on either side, one after another as far as I can see. All have gardens and parks and walks going down to the ocean.

Tuesday evening June 13

Now we are in New York and I am sitting in a hotel room as I write this. Going through Ellis Island[2] was not as bad as we all thought it would be. Everybody was nervous about it, but it was relatively easy. We started up the Bay and had breakfast, and I got a letter from Mr. Moldenhaver. He said he could easily get me a job on a farm if I wanted that, for about 25 dollars a month, plus keep. He is a high official in the State Agricultural Department and he had been transferred from New York to Albany. That is, I was told, about 10 hours by riverboat from New York. We reached Hoboken after about 1 hour and had to wait some time for the baggage to be unloaded and for all the Americans to get off.

We immigrants were put on a small ferry to Ellis Island, where my eyes were examined, the luggage inspected and I had to show that I had $50.00. I had it in my pocket so that went well. Then I was put on another ferryboat that took us to Battery Park in lower Manhattan.

We were a whole bunch of Danish immigrants, and I got talking to a Missionary Petersen who told me of a hotel I could go to. He also introduced me to another Danish man and son named Christiansen who were also looking for a hotel.

The older Christiansen had a farm in Nebraska. He had it rented out on shares to someone so he could take this trip to Denmark and get his son. The son was a telegrapher and had never been to America before, so he was as green as I was, but his father knew his way around. He was also going to Albany to talk to Mr. Moldenhaver as he was interested in buying a farm in New York State, then go to Nebraska and sell his farm there. Missionary Petersen got lost in the crowd but then it was time to get off the ferryboat.

---

2   More information about Ellis Island at the end of the letters

All the immigrants going farther West had big badges pinned on their chests with the name of the place they were going. An officer from the ship herded them together and took charge to get them to the train station and put them on the right train. The rest of us were left to find our own way.

The Christiansens and I walked up the street after collecting our luggage, and we saw this hotel named Swedish Mission Hotel. We went in and got a room for the three of us for $1.00 each per night, including food. (The room itself was 40 cents.)

The people in this hotel spoke Swedish and understood us all right. The rooms were dirty, but we couldn't afford to pay more, so we stayed. It was about 2 p.m., so we had something to eat in the dining room and then took a walk to look over the neighborhood. It looks like a dirty city and the cars are going very fast. I saw a lot of horses and wagons loaded so the horses could hardly pull them. Streetcars are racing down the streets; they are much bigger and longer than in Copenhagen. Electric trains are running overhead on bridges built right down the middle of the street. They go fast and make a racket, and disappear around the corner. It looks dangerous. I am afraid they may run off the track and fall down in the street.

We were on Wall Street and saw some banks and some of the highest buildings; they don't look that high, but they are. The highest building in the world is here, it has 58 floors above the street and 8 floors below street level.[3] This was a long day. I mailed all my letters to you, but I don't know how soon you will get them with that war going on. I hope you don't get in it. It is still Tuesday evening and my first day here.

Love Haldor

---

3 This is most likely the Woolworth Building Built in 1913.

**Wednesday June 14, 7 a.m.
Water Street no. 5, New York City**

That is my address here and I slept here for the first time. I am planning to leave and go to Albany, New York with the Christiansens on the riverboat in a day or two. I got a letter from Mr. Brown in New South Berlin, near Oneonta. It was sent here from the ship's office. I can't understand how they know I am here. Mr. Brown has a farm and invited me to come and visit him. He can get me a job, but his place is not on the way to Albany, so I will go to Albany first and talk with Mr. Moldenhaver. Now, I will mail this today and send you my address when I get settled somewhere.

Love to all, Haldor

**Friday June 16.
on board steamer "Hendrick Hudson"**

I am now on the riverboat going to Albany. I was in New York City two days and used the time to see as much as I could of the city. I am here to see the country, but on $50.00, I have to find work too. New York is a big place and it would take a long time to really see everything. I have been on the subway train and the elevated train, been over the Brooklyn Bridge and on ferryboats and found my way around all right. The young Christiansen goes with me and we talk English to the policemen, and they take our arms and lead us to the subway entrance, tell us how to get there and sometimes tell the conductor where to let us off.

The traffic is terrible. The streets are undermined with tunnels where the subway trains rumble under your feet. The elevated trains are over your head; the streetcars in the street are fairly slow on account of the traffic. The subway stations underground have big platforms and some places have entrances to stores and buildings that have several underground levels. Several tracks run here and the trains come fast and stop suddenly, and all the doors slide open. People come out and others fight to get in; if you get in a crowd, you are forced along into the train, the doors slam shut and the train is off again in 1/2 minute. For 5 cents you pay to go all over New York and back again if you want to. The trains are electric and are made up of 5-7 long cars. The seats are along the sides and you sit facing the people on the opposite side. A broad space is in between for standing. There are no doors between the cars and you can see from one end of the train to the other. The train starts so fast that you have to hang on to your seat to keep from sliding. There is a train about every three minutes. The elevated train is about the same and they run in a height from 2nd floor to as high as the 6th floor, and in places they go underground. There are usually four tracks, two in each direction. The street underneath is dark and the houses are shaking when the trains go by.

The view from the Brooklyn Bridge is wonderful. I took the train over the Bridge, then got off so I could walk back over it. I was then in Brooklyn, and the first train stop was some distance from the Bridge, so I got lost in the streets and had to ask for directions. The street was filled with Negroes, some light and some dark, so I must have been in a Negro section of the city. We do not see any Negroes in Denmark, so to me it was an unusual sight; Negro men, women and children playing in the street, and Negroes running the stores. I even saw a Negro family in a beautiful new car, driving down the street. I have also been in Central Park in the center of Manhattan, but that park is so big I couldn't walk to the other end, where the Harlem Section of the city is (that is also mostly Negroes living there). The park is full of squirrels and they are almost tame. There are big ponds and groups of rocks, flowerbeds and a few stands that sell soft drinks and ice cream. There are plenty of roads where you see rich people drive cars, or beautiful horses and carriages with a coachman and another man on the front seat in full uniform. We found a big museum on one side of the park and there we saw big expensive paintings, sculptures and many things from all over the world. We were tired from walking around all day, so we went back to the hotel, as we had to get up early in the morning and get to the riverboat. The hotel we stayed at in New York, we found out, is run by the Swedish church for the benefit of the immigrants who are coming by the shipload every day - and it was real cheap. It cost us 40 cents a day for a bed, 10 cents for morning coffee and a bun, 30 cents for a dinner and 25 cents for supper. The food is not very good. I saw people buying something they called "hamburg" - it was two pieces of bread with a piece of chopped beef between. There was no gravy, but they poured some kind of tomato sauce on it (it said "ketchup" on the bottle); but I would like gravy. The bread is white only and you get a small pat of butter in the middle. Always two slices for a sandwich, and there is no pumpernickel or French bread.

Our ticket to Albany, on the boat I am now on, cost us $2.00, and we had the run of the whole boat's four floors. An orchestra was playing most of the time and the salons were nice with heavy, thick rugs on the floor, and red chairs with high backs you can lay back in and relax or sleep. We left New York at 8:40 a.m. and are due in Albany at 6:10 p.m. (it is about 150 miles from New York due north on the Hudson River). I think it is an expensive trip, but it is a beautiful ride. We are sailing between tree-covered mountains and on one side runs the railroad tracks. We saw trains going over bridges high over the river, through tunnels and on tracks in the river on dams built from fill taken from the tunnels. I saw a train so long I was amazed and I counted 97 cars. It passed over the head of us on a bridge and then disappeared in a tunnel.

I am traveling with the Christiansens and we all got a package of food when we left the hotel. We ate that early. There were two sandwiches for each and we drank water with them, and we were afraid to buy anything on the boat, as the people in the hotel told us everything on the boat was very expensive. The sandwiches had to last us all day and so now we're already hungry before we reach Albany.

Mr. Christiansen is also going to talk with Mr. Moldenhaver in Albany before going to Nebraska. I hear that on account of the war in Europe there is plenty of work here, as America is exporting all kinds of material to France and England. So there is plenty of work in the cities and in the country.

This is all for now, as we are getting close to Albany, and I will mail the letters there.

The best to all,

Haldor

CHAPTER THREE

Finding A Job

Saturday June 17
Albany 10:00 p.m.

I have been here in Albany since yesterday. We got here about 6 p.m. and we (Christiansen and I) talked with Mr. Moldenhaver. He has a job for me on a big fruit farm in Kinderhook, owned by a wealthy American from New York, his name is Ogden. He told me that another Danish man who he got a job for two months ago just left to go to New York on another job, so now I get that chance. Here is plenty of work and so Mr. Moldenhaver says I can try it and if I don't like it, it will be easy to find something else. I am going to get $25.00 per month, and also room and board.

Today we went on a four hour trip in a State car with Mr. Moldenhaver and the Christiansens, who were looking at farms to buy. The farms look entirely different from farms in Denmark. At first, the farms looked as if they were not plowed, and were used for nothing but grass, and you see trees and bushes all over the fields. There seems to be plenty of trees and woods all over the place. I think every farm has a lot of land in the woods and you see mostly wooden houses. They look good if they are kept up with repair and white paint, but you also see many in bad repair and unpainted.

The landscape is beautiful and is a lush green, but the unpainted wooden houses look bad and give an impression of poverty. Most houses have a big porch where people sit and relax. Albany is a city of 125.000 people and it is the Capitol City of New York. It is a nice city and much cleaner than New York City. Even the streets get washed every night when a water wagon comes through and flushes the street clean. In New York City they did that too, but the streets were so uneven that the water could not run off. It made puddles that you had to try to avoid or get wet feet. The sidewalks here are even and well-kept; in New York the sidewalks were lumpy and often 12 to 15 inches above the street and were difficult for people to get on. Often pipes and other building materials were piled across the walk, but here all is kept nice. In New York City, I saw an unusual sight that I forgot to tell about; an airplane flew low over the city and everyone stopped to look at it, because it was a dangerous stunt. But he made it and went out of sight.

Everybody seems to be in a hurry; the freight wagons are overloaded and the poor horses can hardly pull them. I saw one team and wagon stalled and the horses couldn't get it going again. They were right in the middle of the street on the streetcar track. A streetcar came and couldn't get by, and a shouting match started. Then the driver of the streetcar got off and started waving his arms at the wagon driver. Finally they found a remedy. The streetcar driver drove the streetcar against the wagon and pushed it so the horses could go. Everything has to be done fast and the work is sloppy looking.

They have places where you can buy a glass of beer for 5 cents and you can get a good size sandwich for free, usually a slice of ham between two slices of bread. Some places give you a clam roll or other food they can trim off.

Everything is supposed to go fast here, but I still see workmen standing around talking with hands in their pockets. People sit in the subway in New York reading the small newspapers and then throw them on the floor before leaving, and the newsboys are selling papers running through the trains. The American people like sweets a lot and there are stands along the street selling ice cream in cones and cake with strawberries and cream poured over the cake. That tastes good. I miss the Danish bread and pumpernickel, since leaving the steamship, I have only seen that white bread and some rolls.

It is still beautiful weather but I wear a top hat for the comfort even when the sun doesn't shine. It gets dark early in the evening shortly after 8 p.m. and I long for the long, light evenings in Denmark.

I told you I had a letter and invitation from Brown and his wife Elizabeth. She is our dentist's daughter and I know them from Denmark, so I told Mr. Moldenhaver about the letter and he said that he didn't think they were too well off and Mrs. Brown was a bit off her rocker, as he had been told by Mr. Brown's brother, who had a farm right next to them. So, I said I didn't know them that well, but they gave me a nice invitation.

Tomorrow, I go to my new job, and the address is :

>Alfred Ogden
>Kinderhook Albany
>New York State

When we arrived here in Albany yesterday, Mr. Moldenhaver sent us to a boarding house where we stay now. The lady that runs it has a daughter about 16-18 years old. She offered to show us around the city, so young Christiansen and I asked her to go to a picture show with us. She seemed eager to go so we did that after supper. We saw a good show for 10 cents each. I will mail this letter before leaving and I have to say good-bye to the Christiansens as they are going out west to their farm.

Love to all, Haldor

June 19. 1916

I have now had my first day here on my new job. Mr. Moldenhaver thinks I am interested in buying a farm, so I didn't tell him I wasn't, but I suppose they will soon find out I am not a farmer. Mr. Moldenhaver also said there already was one Danish man working here, but I found out he left last week and went to New York City, so I am taking his job. But, I will start from the beginning...

I got here from Albany about 4 p.m. after riding for about one hour on what was called a Trolley Line. It is nothing but an electric streetcar built like a tram car, running like a train through the countryside, with stations and stops every so often. The trolley runs about one car every hour. I got off at Kinderhook and walked to Ogden's farm, about 15 minutes away. The farm is about 400 acres and Mr. Ogden is a man about 30-35 years old and is married. I was shown to a nice, white well-kept house, and a man was sitting on the porch in a rocking chair with his feet on the porch railing. I asked for Mr. Ogden, and the man said "Mr. Ogden lived in the big house behind the trees there, but if I was the man they expected from Mr. Moldenhaver, I could put my suitcase down and take a chair, because this was the place at which I was to room and eat." I couldn't understand what else he said, and I tried to say something, but he didn't understand me. In the city, I could make myself understood, but not here. Maybe they are not used to foreigners talking broken English. He kept saying "I don't understand you", so maybe he doesn't understand English. But I could understand some of what he said. He told me he worked on the farm and today, being Sunday, he had only to go and feed the horses, so I could go with him to the horses soon.

After a while, he motioned to me and we started walking on a path through a small clump of trees and there was a big building where he said Mr. Ogden lived. We walked past it and got to the stable, he fed the horses and the chickens in another building and I thought I now could talk with Mr. Ogden, but he took me back to the small house, and still no Mr. Ogden. It looked to me like this man was all alone in the house and I began to wonder if he also was the cook, but we sat down again on the porch and smoked our pipes, and I got more and more hungry, but we waited.

Then a car came up the driveway at about 7 p.m. It stopped in front of the porch. I thought, that must be Mr. Ogden, but out came a man with one leg in a cast, then a woman (both were in their late 30's) and finally a girl about 25 and then three children. They all went across the porch and into the house. I and my friend (he was a man about 50) just kept on rocking and smoking. He said nothing and I knew it was useless for me to ask questions. Then after a while we were told to come in and eat supper (The woman said "Supper is ready") so we went in the kitchen where a big table was set. There were stewed potatoes and beans, bread and butter. Every place setting had a small dish with something that looked like rice, but it had no taste - and then water and tea. The bread was the usual white bread and that was our supper. At 9 p.m. we went to bed. I was shown to my room under the roof, but a nice room with a double bed and shining clean with white sheets and two blankets. No feather beds or duvets here, they are not used in this country. There is also a stand with a big water pitcher and a basin to wash myself in, a closet for my clothing, one chair and a straw rug on the floor, so it looked really good. At 5 a.m., I was called to get up and the other man, my friend from yesterday and I walked up to the stables and I was put to work currycombing horses and feeding them and some pigs; it was then 6 a.m. and we walked back to the house to get our breakfast. That was a copy of our supper the night before. I think I am staying with the foreman, but I am not sure. Because of his broken leg, he doesn't go to work and he doesn't understand English when I talk to him, but I understand him. About 7 a.m. after breakfast, we walked back to the farm and I met four others who also work here, so we are six men in all.

Then I was introduced to Mr. Ogden. He gave me a scythe and asked me if I could use it. I said I could, and he told me to cut the grass around the trees in the orchard. About half of the 400 acres is planted with fruit trees, and the other part is mostly grass and some corn. Another man was cutting grass with a machine and a team of horses between the fruit trees that were planted in neat rows, and I cut where the machines couldn't get too close to the trees. I worked at that all forenoon and 12 noon we went home to dinner. I was looking forward to a good meal, and we got potatoes and fried pork, a piece of cake and tea. It was a long stretch from 6 a.m. breakfast, and now it started to rain and after dinner we cleaned and swept up the upstairs floor of the barn. Then we went to another barn about five minutes walk down the lane; that was the cow barn. A family lives in a house there - the man takes care of the cows. There are eight cows so that is not much, but we had to use a wheelbarrow to clean out a round towerlike building called a silo. Some cut-up cornstalks were fermenting there, and it is suppose to be good for the cows.

The cows were all out in a fenced field eating grass so we just cleaned out the silo as the cows didn't need it now. We put it out to be used for fertilizer. In the fall the silo will be filled again with a fresh supply of food for the cows all winter.

It was a long working day, but no one rushes around and the men will stop and roll a handmade cigarette and smoke it. It is surprising to see how some can roll a perfect cigarette. When they get good and ready they will go back to work. If Mr. Ogden comes by they will talk with him and continue smoking until they are ready to start working again.

Mr. Ogden has two automobiles, his wife uses one, a small one, and Mr. Ogden has a nice fancy Cadillac. There is also another old car we use to go for supplies in town. I think Mrs. Ogden has the chickens here. I saw her load a couple of big boxes filled with eggs in her car and drive off to town. She must sell them there. You see quite a few automobiles here, and you can hear them blowing their horns down on the road, even at night. We work here 'til 5 p.m. and after that we feed the horses and chickens before going home to supper at six o'clock.

My hands were full of blisters after the first day of work so they hurt, but I am staying and I have to work one month before I get my first wages of 25 dollars, then I will be rich again. I am in Kinderhook and that is a good ways from Albany, so my address is Kinderhook, New York and not Albany Kinderhook as I first told you. If you already have sent a letter to Albany it is all right, I will still get it.

So, that was my first day here, and as all mail is censored and delayed on account of the war, I can't expect to hear from you for a couple of months. I long to hear how everyone is doing. I hope grandmother is well again. Now you, father and mother, will soon have your silver anniversary.

The best to all, Haldor

July 19. 1916
Kinderhook, New York

It is about three weeks since I wrote my last letter to you, but I sent out some picture post cards to you and others, so I will use the time today, Sunday, to write to you. It has been hot here lately and the last two days the thermometer has gone over 90 degrees, as high as 95 degrees even in the shade, so it was difficult to do any work. The water would run off of us whether we worked or rested.

Today is slightly better as the sun is not out so I hope for rain. The climate here is different from Denmark. The sun is shining about every day and we may get 1 or 2 rainy days every week, usually thunder showers and then the sun comes out again hot and bright. Usually there is no wind to speak of. I think working on a farm is harder than working in the city, but Mr. Ogden doesn't push anyone. It is just that everything is heavy and hard to do. Like now, we are in the middle of haying and that is hard work when the temperature is over 90°. Here is about 100 to 150 acres in grass and that is cut as food for the cows and horses. We have five horses in the stable, but the cows are out in a fenced in field. A fenced in road leads to the cow barn and the cows are trained to come home to the barn every evening to be milked. They stay in the barn all night and get milked again in the morning before they are let out and they follow the fenced road out to the field by themselves so nobody has to take them there. At night, they again show up at the door to get in the stable. The milk is well taken care of. The milk from every cow is weighed and cooled on ice. Then the milk is put through a centrifuge that works by electric motor. The cream is put on ice and later taken to Kinderhook and sold. The thin skimmed milk is fed to the pigs. In the winter, the cows get cut up corn stalks. They are planted between the young fruit trees and we also have a small field with corn. When we don't work with the hay, we clean between the rows of corn with a cultivator pulled by one horse. The corn stalks are cut and put in the silo in the fall to be used during the winter. We also have a piece of land with potatoes. After the grass is cut it is dried for about 24 hours, then turned over with a machine and dried some more. It is finally raked up in rows, and then a machine behind a wagon rakes it up and puts it on the wagon. It takes 3 men to operate that outfit; one to drive the horses and two to place the loose hay around the sides and in the middle of the wagon so you can have a nice big load on the wagon. Then you drive it to the barn where another machine grabs the load of hay in about 4 or 5 grabs and slides it in the barn. I have worked on the hay for about 2 weeks now and it will take another 2 or 3 weeks before we are done.

When it rains or it is damp we have another job going. Mr. Ogden has had a siding from the trolley line put on his land and now we are building a packing house for the apples. The fruit will be sorted and packed in boxes and barrels and then shipped first to New York and from there to anyplace in the world and as Mr. Ogden said maybe some end up in Denmark. We are digging the trench for the foundation. Mr. Ogden usually takes us there in an automobile with our shovels and sometimes I drive as Mr. Ogden works sometimes with us. He has, by himself, dug a well 20 feet deep, he also helps with hay now and then.

Saturday afternoon is free time for us so we can get to town and shop if we want to. I wrote to you about the Danish man that worked here. They told me he left Saturday, and I came on Sunday. He went to New York City. He had been here only 2 weeks when somebody in New York got him a job there for 2 dollars per day and he didn't like being a farmer. I doubt if it was any better because he probably had to pay 1 dollar per day for board and room. I have heard about something better. I am told the automobile factories in Detroit are paying as high as 5 dollars a day and I would like very much to go there and try that. I am here to see the country and that would be a change. I asked Mr. Ogden about it and he said they do pay 5 dollars a day, but I would have to get some experience first so I would not get it right away. I have been thinking about it and now I told Mr. Ogden I would leave and go to Detroit on Aug. 18th,

I have been here two months. Mr. Ogden asked me if I know a Danish man that would like to come to work here, but I don't know anybody, so Mr. Ogden is going to contact Mr. Moldenhaver. Mr. Ogden still thinks I am interested in eventually buying a farm so he told me something about this farm. It was run down when he got it 3 years ago for $22,000.00 and there are 432 acres with about 75 acres in woods. When he came here he got very little hay and he had to fertilize and lime the land at a big expense and now he gets a good crop of hay and corn. The farmers use mules in place of horses on most farms. They are stronger and tougher and can live on less food but cost more than horses. A good horse costs 400 - 500 dollars.

Kinderhook is a beautiful little town and it takes about 20 minutes to walk into town. I have been there about every Saturday evening. Then the stores are open. Yesterday I bought a knife, as I lost the one I had in the hay, and also ink. Kinderhook is a small town, but is located in a beautiful part of the country and there are beautiful houses built of wood with porches on the front and all painted white.

Every Saturday evening they have a concert on the bandstand in the middle of the square. It seems everyone from the farms around comes in to shop and hear the music so there are a lot of people and cars here. I counted 30 cars parked around the square and after a music number from the orchestra they would all blow their horns to show they enjoyed the effort of the musicians. Most every farm has a car of some sort, some only an old broken down Ford, but if they run they come to town Saturday evening. Young people also buy cars, if they have 100 dollars they can get one. From my window in my room I can see over the fields; but in Denmark you see no trees or bushes in the fields, the whole farm is plowed and under cultivation, here you see trees and bushes and orchards and woods and very often I can see mountains in a haze, at times they are clear. That is the Catskill Mountains about 50 miles from here.

I was very surprised to see little insects fly around like sparks from a fire. They will light up. There are thousands of them around in the evening, it is a beautiful sight. I am told that they are called lightning bugs and some people call them fire flies. I have now been here three weeks and my hands are getting tough - they don't blister and hurt anymore so I am getting to be a farmer and I think I am doing all right and I like it here so far. No mail yet. That is all for now.

Love to all, Haldor

CHAPTER FOUR

A New Job

Aug. 18, 1916 evening
Kinderhook N.Y.

Dear all, I hope you get this letter in time for Dad's birthday Sept. 13, but you never know. I have not had a letter from you yet and I know you have sent some, but that war is disrupting the mails. Anyway, I am sending a happy birthday to you. Tomorrow is my birthday, but it will be like any other day. As you can see, I am still in Kinderhook. I told Mr. Ogden, I was leaving to go to Detroit, but since then things have changed. Now I have to stay here another month until Sept. 18 and I will tell you how that came about. I like Mr. Ogden very much and I trust him. He is a good man and I was not surprised when he called me aside and said he had something to tell me. He asked me if

I had a job waiting for me in Detroit. If not then he had something I might like and he would like very much to do something for me. He has a friend in Chatham, a millionaire, an old man and is a retired U.S. Marshal (appointed by President Ulysses S. Grant) and Ex. New York State Insurance Commissioner called Louis Payn[4]. Chatham is about 8-10 miles from Kinderhook and Mr. Payn had just made up his mind to buy an automobile and he needed someone to drive for him, so if I would like that job, Mr. Ogden would help me get it. Mr. Payn has 22 horses, some of them racehorses, some for driving and he has always used horses and never automobiles. He didn't like them very much and he is over 70 years old, but he has a younger wife and she talked him into buying an automobile. It is to be an enormously fancy and expensive automobile, that will cost $6,000 dollars and he wanted someone he could trust to drive it and take care of it, someone that doesn't drink. Mr. Ogden said he doesn't like anybody that drinks. I was told by one of the hands that he doesn't like drinking because he has a son living in New York City that drinks too much and he is angry about that. Mr. Ogden would take me to see Mr. Payn. If I stayed with him, I could get a good recommendation as Mr. Payn was known all over the country and did some traveling. It sounded good to me and he also said I could get more pay than I got now working on the farm. So I said O.K. and the same afternoon Mr. Ogden drove over to Chatham to talk to Mr. Payn just to see about this job for me. He didn't find Mr. Payn home, but his wife was there and she said it would be all right, but she would have Mr. Payn telephone Mr. Ogden so he could bring me there again. So this afternoon, I was in the orchard picking pears and Mrs. Payn telephoned for us to come, I had to go home and get dressed to go with Mr. Ogden to Chatham to talk to the millionaire Mr. Payn. Mr. Ogden asked me to drive for him over there and we stopped to pick up Mr. Payn at his big house and we took him for a trip around the neighborhood. Mr. Payn said I did all right

---

4   More information about Louis Payn at the end of the letters

and he would hire me and pay me 35 dollars a month and also board and room somewhere else. But he wouldn't get the automobile until the end of September so it was decided that I stay with Mr. Ogden until September 18th. That is another month. Mr. Ogden was glad to keep me as the fruit picking season was coming. So, on Sept. 18th, I will move to Chatham and then I have to go to New York and get the automobile at the dealer, I am then to stay in New York a week or 10 days and get to know the working of the car and how to take care of it, and also get used to driving it. I will also have to get a chauffeur's, license. No license is required to drive your own car, but as a chauffeur, I will need one.

Residence of the Hon. Louis F. Payn, Chatham, N. Y.

Stupplebeen's Boarding House

On the way home from Chatham, Mr. Ogden held a nice little speech for me. He said he trusted me to do my best for Mr. Payn and he knew I could be trusted. That is why he did that for me and he thought I would be satisfied there and Mr. Payn satisfied with me also. Mr. Payn goes to Bermuda in the winter time, as he has a house there and he will probably take me with him.

I like to travel and see as much as possible while I am here so I liked that. Bermuda is an island in the Atlantic two days sailing from New York. They have no winter there. Bananas and oranges grow in the garden and you can pick strawberries in February. They don't use the auto there as they are not allowed to drive them on the roads there so Mr. Payn is bringing four horses there to use and his Negro driver to take care of them and drive for him. I am getting worried about getting a chauffeur's license so Mr. Ogden said he would go to Albany and find out about that as you are suppose to be able to speak and read English to get it.

Bermuda is an English Island under an English Governor. This was a long day and tomorrow is my birthday. I will be 24 and I long to hear from you as it is soon three months since I left Denmark and said good-bye to you all. My mail must soon be here.

Love to all,

Haldor

Aug. 20, 1916
Kinderhook N.Y.

Dear All,

It was a wonderful birthday present. I got the first batch of mail from you. Wasn't that a wonderful coincidence? The mailman came and there was that big blue envelope that Dad always uses and inside was a letter from each of you. It was mailed on July 17 so it took just one month to get here. I also got a roll of newspapers you mailed July 25 and some postcards from Solveig[5] mailed July 21 from Lyngby. Thanks for all of it and I am glad to hear you are alright and well, The papers are good to read and the children here like to try to figure out the comics since it is the same figures we have in the papers here.

Just keep the letters coming and mail them to me here in Kinderhook as I don't know my address in Chatham and when I move I will have my mail forwarded to me there. We get mail here once every day. The mailman comes in an automobile now in the summertime, but in the winter he uses a wagon or a sled as a lot of snow falls and there is nothing like snowplowing as it is usually too much and hopeless so you see no automobiles outside the big cities, only big trucks can get through. we are now digging potatoes and have started to pick apples. Potatoes are sold in Kinderhook by the bushel and we get 1 dollar for them. That is a high price this year, but they also are fine potatoes. I now look forward to getting my next letter from you.

Love Haldor

---

5   Solveig is Haldor's younger sister

Sept. 2, 1916
Kinderhook, N.Y.

Thanks for the letters; I got more since writing my last letter. I got the letters from Adda, Soren [6], Solveig and Dad and a couple of cards sent to me during your trip to Odden. I wish I could have been with you on that trip, but that can't be, so I am looking forward to moving to Chatham and then my trip to New York City to pick up that expensive automobile.

It is a new, almost experimental auto and there are none like it around. That is why I have to go to the factory in New York and learn all about it. Mr. Ogden is using me as a chauffeur now and last Sunday, I drove him and Mrs. Ogden to Lenox and then to Pittsfield, Massachusetts. That was a nice trip. They went to visit Mr. Ogden's mother. She is a widow and has 9 million dollars. She travels a lot, mostly by automobile. She has a chauffeur and Mr. Ogden asked him to look after me as I was a foreigner and still didn't speak English well, so he came and helped me get something to eat. Mr. Ogden's mother was staying in a big hotel in Lenox and we went to the dining room where I got a menu stuck in my hand, but I couldn't read it. This was the first time I ate in a real restaurant and I had to take the same dinner my partner ordered. After I got it, I didn't know what it was, a big brown burned thing on my plate turned out to be a potato. The chauffeur told me it was baked, but I had never seen that before. It was good and so was the rest of the dinner. The meat was beef and I liked it. I was glad I had help. We didn't pay for anything, it went on Ogden's bill. The chauffeur told me he got $100.00 a month.. He told me also that he was married, and had bought a little house on a farm about 14 acres on Long Island near his work, but he wasn't home as much as he liked and this lady was always going someplace and he had to go too. On trips, she would pay for his expenses, but home he lived with his family in his house. After dinner, we took a trip in Mr. Ogden's auto as he was going to stay all afternoon and he told us we could go, so

---

6   Adda is Haldor's older sister and Soren is her husband

we went to Pittsfield, a beautiful little city, and the road from Lenox ran through beautiful country with mountains and woods.

His lady lives on Long Island between trips in the winter. She lives mostly in New York City. Sometimes she goes to Florida, but it is a rough trip there with the ship from New York. He said he had been in every major city in the United States and Canada with her and she is 72 years old. We went back to Lenox, and later I drove back to Kinderhook. Today, I went to the photographer to have my picture taken for my chauffeur's license, as I will have to try to get it soon. I am getting more used to the food here, but I still miss some of the Danish dishes, especially the Danish pastries and the pumpernickel. We get something called pie - it is real good sometimes, but it is not pastry. I would also like some oatmeal in the morning, but I get some dry stuff with milk on. I think they can get oatmeal here and it is so good for your stomach, but it probably takes too much time to make it. I am enclosing a postcard to Aunt Nora, please give her that. When I get my photographs, I will send you some.

The weather is now better as it is not so hot. You can now sit in the sun, like we used to do home and not try to get in the shade, which we did all summer. Only the night gets quite cold, almost down near freezing. I have trouble understanding the thermometer here. I wonder if Dad can explain it so I can figure it over in Centigrade degrees. I will write again when I get to Chatham or New York City.

Love,

Haldor

Sept. 19, 1916
New York City

Dear Dad and Mom.

I am now in New York City, sent here by Mr. Payn to pick up the new auto. I got over to Chatham last Sunday and got directed to a boarding house run by Mr. and Mrs. Stupplebeen. Mr. Stupplebeen works for Mr. Payn as a sort of manager on the estate and looks after the grounds and the gardens. I waited until Monday afternoon before meeting Mr. Payn again, but now I am getting second thoughts about this job. Mr. Payn told me he doesn't stay here in the wintertime, and an auto is useless then anyway, as the roads are not plowed free of snow. He goes to Bermuda where he has an estate or anyway a big house and gardens. If I wanted to go there with him, he would take me and I could work in the garden. He also said he could not pay me $35.00 a month there as the wages generally were very low in Bermuda and he would have to pay my ticket there and back and I would not be working as a chauffeur. I didn't like that too well, but I was anxious to get that trip and had looked forward to it. Then Mrs. Payn suggested they pay me $35.00 but I take care of my own food and I could room over the stables where the coachman and the stable boy lived. Well, I was willing to go then and they said we would all leave at the end of November and stay until May 1st. I got the impression Mr. Payn was a little tight with his money, but his wife was nice. So, I am now set for the winter and by next spring, I can still go to Detroit, if I want to. I then got my orders about going to New York City and Mr. Payn gave me some money for expenses and told me how to get there. I then talked to the coachman. He's a big Negro and he had been to Bermuda before with them, also, the stable boy is going, he is a young Negro. They said they had a stove there to cook on, and we could cook our own meals, as it would cost 64 cents a week to eat with a nearby farmer and the food was lousy. The farmers there have small plots of land and raise mostly onions and they are of Portuguese descent.

I left Chatham last night at 6 p.m. with the train to Hudson and from there with the riverboat to New York. Mr. Payn had arranged for a stateroom for me and I slept on the riverboat until we got to New York City at 8:30 a.m., 2 hours behind schedule, so it took me 14 hours to get there. I don't know about hotels here so I went to the Swedish hotel I was in before and I got a room there with two Danish men that have been here two weeks. I have not seen them yet as they are out to work somewhere. They are painters.

Today, there is a ship from Denmark, so the hotel expects more Danish emigrants to check in. I am getting along better with the language and can usually make myself understood and also understand what is said to me. (Later) I have now been out to the factory to look at the automobile. They are building an enclosed back seat with windows in the doors that can be turned down to open. There is a big glass to the front, behind the driver so I will be sitting out in the open. It is an immense big auto with a 6 cyl. motor that turns a dynamo, that produces electricity, that is directed to electric motors, that do the actual work of pulling the automobile ahead. A lever on the steering wheel directs the electricity, more or less, to the wheels. Almost like a streetcar. The name of the automobile is Owen-Magnetic[7] and it is luxurious.

Several Danish people came with the ship today and are staying here. I met some and also my two Danish painters, I share the room with. I was so happy about being able to talk Danish again and be understood, but I am disgusted with myself for mixing English words into my Danish, so I must have picked up a lot of English.

My two painters are working a few days painting a fence. One is a house painter and the other is a landscape and portrait artist, but he can also paint fences. This was a long and full day and I am going to bed. Goodnight and love to all.

Hal

Sept. 26, 1916
New York City

---

[7] See end of letters for more information on the Owen-Magnetic automobile.

I am still here in New York City and it looks like I will have to stay for a while. Now they tell me, I can't get the car for about two weeks more, but they have another demonstrator, I can take out for one or two hours every day to get used to driving it.

I can't understand why Mr. Payn sent me here, when it takes so long. I have been here one week now and I am really just wasting my time here doing nothing. I have been out with my painter friend and see him paint a landscape from Central Park. He had to get a permit to set up his easel in the park. He has gone to school in Copenhagen "Art school" and has painted some nice paintings but has not sold any. His friend is painting for a Swedish contractor and is getting a weekly wage so he is making out much better. The artist says he is not going to paint fences and doors. That is not for him.

America is a big country as everybody knows, but you still can meet people you know on the street. The other day when I was walking down the street, all of a sudden I hear "Is that Haldor?" When I looked up, there was a man about 25 year's old standing looking at me. I didn't recognize him but I said he was right. I was Haldor so he said "We went to high school together in Frederikssund, and my brother Hans has been to your parents' house in Denmark visiting". He said, he had been in USA 5 years and he had just been in the Scandinavian American S/S Line office and got a ticket to go home to Denmark for a visit. Then I remembered him and had a nice talk with him. Then the next day, after I had taken my daily auto trip in the new car in the park, I was on my way home walking down 5th. Ave. to get the elevated train to the hotel, and then I saw a girl I knew from the ship coming over. Her name was Elna and I talked with her for a while. She had a job with a family on Lenox Ave. The girl was Finnish and we tried to talk English. It didn't go too good so we soon said good-bye.

Yesterday, I was in a skyscraper building, it had 24 floors[8] and I was there with my painter friend. He had to go there about his painting permit. We went way up to the 12th floor and there was a good view. Someday, I will go all the way up to the top and see over the city. I am feeling fine and I hope all of you home are well. I expect there will be letters for me when I get back to Chatham. I am still not sure I like this job and I still have no chauffeur's license. I think I better go and see about getting it.

I met a young Danish man and he said, he had been here two months and he only had $3.00 left. He acted funny and would laugh when he eats and he doesn't know what he laughs at He is, I think, feebleminded. He said he gets sick when he works, he has been to doctors and also in the hospital, but they didn't keep him. He can't talk one word of English after two months here. Now he wants to go back home, but he only has the $3.00 so he went to the Danish liner harbored here and leaving in a couple of days and tried to get some work so he could get home. But they would not have him, so I don't know what will happen to him.

Love to all, Haldor

October 5, 1916
New York City

Dear family and all.

As you can see I am still in New York City. I just received some letters, you mailed in August and first week of September. You write about Betty dying and she was Solveig's girlfriend. I don't know her, but that was really bad. Can Solveig take some pictures of Grandmother and our dog Pussi and also everyone else?

---

8   Possibly the New York's City Municipal Building

My roommate the artist has been using my head as a model in a picture he is painting. He is really good, I can't understand why he can't sell any paintings.

I got my chauffeur's driving permit now. I thought this would be a good time to try as I had nothing else to do so I went for the test yesterday with the car. I had to drive around the streets and that was fine, but then there was a written test and they give us 10 questions to answer, each was read loud twice and some, I didn't understand. I asked permission to write my answers in Danish and got it, but I still know at least 4 were wrong so 6 may have been right. Today, I got the license in the mail so I was happy about that.

Haldor's 1916 Chauffeur's License
Front

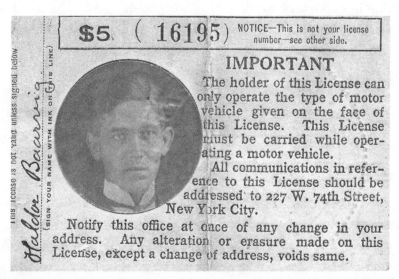

Back

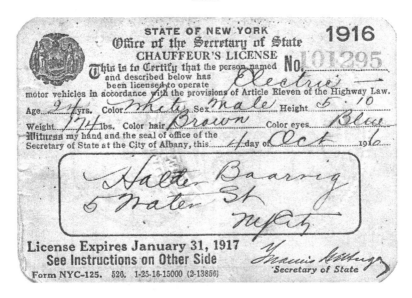

I hope not too many letters disappear on the way over, but I think some do. The automobile is still not ready to go, now they tell me it will be at least another week. This is a long New York trip and I really wish I had a job here so I could stay. It is nice to be with people you can talk to. Saturday my two painters and I went to an automobile race outside New York City on a speedway. The cars had to cover 250 miles on a 2 mile track. It was an oval and the curves at each end were banked so the cars could take them at full speed. The race started at 2:30 p.m. and about 30 cars started. It was over by 5 p.m. the cars had done the 250 miles in 2 1/2 hours., that is about 100 miles per hour. But that was too much for most of them. It didn't look as if they were going that fast, but you could hear a sudden swish as they went by. A Peugeot came in no. 1, Sunbeam was ahead for 100 miles, but had to go out with motor trouble. One caught fire and burned and one turned head over heels with an exploded tire and only 10 made it to the end. It is bedtime now so good night.

Haldor

Lis Clark

October 15, 1916
Chatham, New York

Dear Mom & Dad

As you can see from the heading on this letter, I am again back in Chatham after three weeks in New York mostly sightseeing. Saturday, the 7th, when I came home to the hotel, there was a letter from Mr. Payn asking me to return to Chatham so I got there Sunday. Monday, I was put to work with two other men digging drainage ditches on a low piece of land in Mr. Payn's garden. Mr. Stupplebeen is the overseer or caretaker and I am so tired from digging and sore in all my muscles after a full week of that kind of work, but I have no car here so there is no other work for me. On Tuesday, I am again going to New York City. Now the car is finally ready to travel so they say. Mr. Payn hinted he may buy one more car, an open touring car, except for a top that can be raised or lowered according to the weather. The one we get now is permanently enclosed, it is called a limousine. I also was to a tailor in Chatham and got measured to a uniform.

We are now supposed to leave for Bermuda after the 15th of November so we will not have much time to use the car and I will not see much of the winter here which is very tough, cold and with a lot of snow. The few people that have cars usually put them in the garage by the end of November, jack them up and put blocks under them to take the weight off the tires and leave them there until the snow is melted in the spring. It was still warm in New York 10 days ago when I was there and the cold weather came suddenly and the thermometer fell 40 degrees. in 24 hours. In New York it was 80 degrees and dropped to 40 degrees in the daytime and frost all night.

In Bermuda it is warm all year, around 60 degrees to 70 degrees in the winter and 70 degrees to 80 degrees in the summer. Not much difference between summer and winter. It must be a beautiful and a nice place to spend your winters.

The mail is all fouled up and I have not had any mail in one month until now. Your letter was welcomed and I do not think you can send anything to me for Christmas and I don't need to expect anything, but there is a couple of things you can try to get for me. That is a Danish-English Dictionary and then some newspapers as I can't read the American too well yet. I heard a Danish newspaper is published out west somewhere, but I don't know how to get it and now I am moving to Bermuda anyway. Mr. Payn's estate there is called "Paynhurst" and the address is Hamilton, Bermuda. Send me some Danish pancakes and some of Mom's cookies. Ha try and get them. I am feeling fine.

The best to all, Haldor

Lis Clark

STATE OF NEW YORK
SECRETARY OF STATE'S OFFICE
AUTOMOBILE BUREAU

FRANCIS M. HUGO
SECRETARY OF STATE

NEW YORK CITY

October 25, 1916.

Dear Sir:-

    As one of a rapidly increasing number of motorists, you are interested in this great bureau of the State Government.

    Consider for a moment these figures: From February 1st to September 30, 1916 there were registered in this Office 288545 automobiles, owners and dealers, 93077 chauffeurs, and 23990 motorcycles, for which $2,460,849.75 was received in fees. This is an increase over the corresponding period last year of 38%. There is every indication of an equal or even larger increase during 1917.

    To be able to render to the motor vehicle public prompt and efficient service, I am asking your co-operation in the matter of returning to this office as promptly as possible the enclosed renewal card with required fee.

    I recognize the fact that without your assistance it will be impossible to render the best service. Therefore, permit me to remind you that if you have changed your address since application was last filed, you should notify this office of your old and your new address, including in this notification your present license number.

    Also permit me to remind you that failure to renew your license in any one year means loss of right to renew and obliges you by law to pay original fee of five dollars and take another examination.

    I appreciate most heartily the spirit of good will and co-operation heretofore extended to me, which co-operation has made possible a reduction in administrative expenses of this Bureau of $71,000.00 or from 15% in 1914 to 8% during the current year.

Sincerely yours,

ary of State.

Letter Haldor received from NYS State Automobile Bureau

The letter above is not readable so I am re-writing it. lc

October 25, 1916

Dear Sir:

As one of a rapidly increasing number of motorists, you are interested in this great Bureau of the State Government.

Consider for a moment these figures: From February 1st to September 1st, 1916 there were registered in this Office 288545 automobiles, owners and dealers, 93077 chauffeurs, and 23990 motorcycles for which $2.460.840.75 was received in fees. This is an increase over the corresponding period last year of 38%. There is an indication of an equal or even larger increase during 1917.

In order to render to the motor vehicle public prompt and efficient service, I am asking your co-operation in the matter of returning to this office as promptly as possible the enclosed renewal card with required fee.

I recognize the fact that without your assistance it will be impossible to render the best service. Therefore permit me to remind you that if you have changed your address since application was last filed, you should notify this office of your old and your new address. including in this notification your present license number.

Also permit me to remind you that failure to renew your license in any one year means loss of right to renew and obliges you by law to pay original fee of five dollars and take another examination.

I appreciate most heartily the spirit of good will and co-operation heretofore extended to me, which co-operation has made possible the reduction in administration expenses of this Bureau of $71,015.00or from 19% in 1914 to 9% during the current year.

Sincerely yours,
name not readable
Secretary of State

CHAPTER FIVE

Finally, I Got the New Car

Chatham
October 31, 1916

I went to New York and got the new car. It is beautiful and a salesman came back with me to deliver it to Mr. Payn and I had a nice fast trip down to New York and also a nice trip back to Chatham. We started from New York, (Columbus Circle and Central Park) at 10 a.m. and went by way of Poughkeepsie and Hudson. We drove slow as the roads were bad in places and we had all day to make it about 140 miles to Chatham. At 1 p.m. in Poughkeepsie, we stopped for lunch. The demonstrator salesman and I, started again at 2 p.m.. We got to Chatham at 5 p.m. and delivered the car to Mr. Payn. The next morning we couldn't start it. It was so tight in the motor that we couldn't turn the crank, so the salesman tried to repair it, but it would not go now that it was cold. He had a mechanic come up from New York to fix it and he worked all afternoon and all night until next morning. He took the oil pan down and loosened all the piston rods that were too tight on the crankshaft and by morning, he had the car going again. The man went back to New York and I was nervous about the monster, but I had no more trouble with it. Mr. and Mrs. Payn have had a few short trips to Hudson, Kinderhook, Pittsfield and Ghent. Mrs. Payn likes the car and she said if it wasn't so late in the season, she would like a trip to Montreal, Canada, but now we may get snow any time. I am enclosing a map of New York State so you can see the places I am talking about.

We will soon be going for the winter and it has started to get cold here with frost most every night. Most days are clear and sunshine. We have very little rain. I have a good place to stay and the food is good. I still live with Mr. and Mrs. Stubblebeen. Since, he is the supervisor over the grounds he has to look after one gardener and two men in the stable taking care of four horses and two mules. He sees that the garden is in order and he looks after the central heating in the big house. He also has to raise a few vegetables and some hay for the horses. Mr. Payn is going to build a new stable and garage this winter and spring as we only have an old barn now. Last Saturday, I went to the picture show and I was surprised to see a show I had seen in Denmark. It was "Cabiria". I am enclosing some postage stamps and Christmas stamps. I will also send some from Bermuda. Please send more pictures from home. I like, very much, to get them.

Love to all

Hal

$50 In My Pocket

Hal standing next to the Owen-Magnetic auto

Chatham, New York

Dear All,

I thank you for all the cards and letters I just got. I also got a letter from Marie (Soren's sister) and the first letter from you sent directly to Chatham. I am always so happy to get mail from home, but don't worry about me. I am feeling fine even if I don't look well on the picture I sent, it is the picture that is wrong. I am fine, but I probably have lost a few pounds digging ditches. We eat good here. We have oatmeal for breakfast with milk and sugar, also potatoes and leftover meat and coffee. For dinner potatoes, meat, gravy and a dish with either tomatoes or vegetables, sometimes cooked pears or applesauce, coffee and cake or pie. Then for supper, we again eat meat, potatoes, vegetables sometimes a dish of soup first and then tea. We are about ten minutes from the center of town. I can't take pictures of the room, but I am enclosing a drawing of the room I have. I have a writing desk, a rocking chair, a small table, a clothes closet and a bureau of drawers with a mirror on top. My trunk is at the end of the double bed, nice curtains, a white cover on the bureau, straw rug on the floor and over the bed is a big picture in a gold frame of a farm and a Negro hut along a small creek. The Mr. and Mrs. from the big house in the background are coming across the creek on horseback and waving to the Negroes outside the hut. On the other wall is a picture of a little boy and girl and on the third wall is a picture in frame of three little cats. We have electric lights. My Danish flag is standing on the dresser and the room is on the second floor next to the bathroom with hot and cold running water and a bathtub.

Mr. and Mrs. Stupplebeen have a bedroom on this floor, also their daughter Ann Elizabeth who is 11 years old. Mr. Stupplebeen's mother lives here in the summertime, also another room rented out to two other men working on the railroad. We eat good here and it is a fat family. They look to weigh over 200 pounds each and the girl probably 125-135 pounds. Elizabeth is good at drawing pictures and I am enclosing a drawing of my head she made and it is good.

It doesn't look like we are going to Bermuda right away as I see no signs of packing. But I make more money staying here so it is all right with me, my only concern is your letters may get there before I do.

I got my wages and expenses in New York paid, but I went in the hole on that as I spent some extra money for shows and coffee. I am picking up on my English, I think. I understand about everything they say to me, but I still wish I could read better and talk better. My ear tells me I am talking wrong. I can hear it is wrong, but I still can't do better. I read American children's books I get from Elizabeth, but the adult books I can't read yet.

I am feeling good, but I don't think any Danish people live around here as I haven't met any and I wish I could get a Danish newspaper with Danish writing. I think I am homesick for Denmark and all of you as it is sort of lonesome to have nobody to talk to. I could never think of staying here no matter how good I could live. I would always feel homeless and lonesome and I miss something here we have in Denmark and that is "hygge" (coziness). Of course, I realize if I were born and brought up here and had friends and family here then I would not miss things that I never had. It will be a good deal closer to Christmas by the time this gets to Denmark, but the letters have been coming over faster lately, about three to four weeks. I don't think I will be home for Christmas this year, I can't get the couple of days off, I will need to get there and back.

Love, Hal

Chatham, New York
Nov. 19, 1916

Dear All,

I didn't get any letters this week so I am expecting two letters next week. I told you I had not seen or met any Danes around here but a couple of days ago the coachman came back from town and told me there was a Danish man in Chatham. He was a tailor and had a store there and I had been there shopping, not knowing he was Danish and he didn't know I was Danish. The coachman, Frank, had talked with him about Mr. Payn's new automobile that would take the place of the horses he now had and also about the new man driving it. So it turned out he was Danish and he asked that I come in to see him. I went there the next day and introduced myself. His name was Christensen and he and his brother were running this store and tailor shop. His brother was in the back room and when I went in there to meet him he was sitting cross-legged in the center of an enormous big table sewing and he turned out to be the tailor that made and measured me for my uniform. So I had met him before not knowing he was Danish. We talked and I learned the two brothers were married to Danish girls and now had the finest and best tailor shop and clothing store in Chatham. They were from Jutland and their Danish dialect was still so strong. I could hardly understand them whether they talked Danish or English, but I am still glad there is at least a couple of Danes here.

The weather is getting cold and bad. Monday night it started with a cold rain. Tuesday it was still drizzling and frost so everything was covered with ice. Tuesday afternoon it turned into snow so now we have a thin layer of snow. It is still frost and the water barrel has two inches of ice on top. We have not been digging drainage ditches again, but I volunteered to do it so they could get finished with it before the heavy frost sets in.

No sign, as yet, about our trip to Bermuda. Today, we had fried liver for dinner, it was good. I expect a letter soon and send me a drawing of the new school they are going to build for you. So Marie had a big party and you were all there and had a good time. I went to the store to shop for Mrs. Payn today. Butter costs 35 cent a pound and a quart of milk grade A is 9 cents.

Love to all, Hal.

Sunday Nov. 25, 1916

I have, today, been to church with Mr. & Mrs. Stupplebeen. It is a Lutheran church and tonight we are all going there to a church fair in the basement of the church. We are six going Mr. & Mrs. Stupplebeen, Anna Elizabeth, me and two other men getting room and board here. This afternoon, we were sitting in the parlor talking about how much we weighed, and Mr. Stupplebeen said he weighed 264 pounds and Mrs. Stupplebeen was 214 pounds and Elizabeth was 125 pounds. I don't know how much I weigh but it is less than I weighed at home because of all the hard work. After supper we all went to the church fair. They had music and a short skit of comedy on the stage. They opened the booths for sale of ice cream cones, candy, books, soda water and chances on different things. Most things were donated to the church and the money taken in went to pay the church expenses.

About a month ago, I saw a parade in the street in connection with the presidential election. It was for Hughes. First came an orchestra playing wind instruments, then some people carrying flares with red lights (it was in the evening after dark) then came a goat carrying placards and more people in uniforms walking. The next night, I saw one for Wilson. That started off with the same orchestra marching down Main Street, with the placards and men carrying banners VOTE FOR WILSON. Then one old mule carrying a placard saying, I can do better than Hughes so vote for me. Then came a small wagon pulled by a goat, then people with red coats hollering and screaming. I guess they all had a good time and by the time they got to voting they didn't know who they were voting for.

Lis Clark

WINDSOR THEATRE
CENTRAL SQUARE CHATHAM, N.Y.

MR. J. SISKA, OWNER

PROGRAM FOR WEEK.

Monday, Nov. 20th
"The Dragon" Featuring Margaret Fisher
Pathe Travelogue
Admission 5 and 10c.   Shows 7:15 and 8:45.

Tuesday, Nov. 21th
"A Woman's Fight," Featuring Geraldine
O'Brien and Thurlow Bergen
Whiffle's Custard Date, Comedy
Admission 5 and 10c.   Shows 7:15 and 8:45.

Wednesday, Nov. 22. "The Love Trail"
Giving Them Fits, Pathe Comedy
Admission 5 and 10c.   Shows 7:15 and 8:45.

Thursday's Show to be Announced
Admission 5 and 10c.   Shows 7:15 and 8:45.

Friday, Nov. 24th
Robt. Edeson in "Big Jim Garrity"
Pathe Comedy
Admission 5 and 10c.   Shows 7:15 and 8:45.

Saturday's Show to be Announced

Windsor Theater Program used to write letter on

I have been to the Windsor Theater Picture Show on Central Square in Chatham. Since I have written all over it, I will rewrite it so you can see it better. Stationary is expensive so I used whatever I could find. hb

Monday Nov. 20th
"The Dragon" featuring Margaret Fisher
Pathe Travelogue

Tuesday Nov. 21st
"A Woman's fight" Geraldine O'Brien and
Thurlow Bergen
"Whiffle's Custard Date", comedy

Wednesday Nov. 22nd
"The Love Trail"
Giving them fits, Pathe Comedy

Thursday's show to be announced

Friday Nov. 24th
Robert Edeson in "Big Jim Garrity"
Pathe comedy
admission - Balcony 5 cents-Floor 10 cents
shows at 7:15 and 8:45

**Chatham
Nov. 30, 1916**

Dear Dad and Mom,

It is getting close to Christmas, so I am wishing you all a Merry Christmas and a good New Year. Today is an American holiday. It is Thanksgiving, so I have time to write. I have been on a trip to New York. The car broke down with a broken rear axle. Mr. Payn didn't want anybody around here to repair it, so he sent me to New York to explain at the factory what was wrong and they insisted on sending a mechanic here to fix it. It got to be late and a tough trip for me. They sent us out with an old auto with only one seat for one person, the driver. There was only a wooden box in back with some tools and parts. A board was nailed across the box for me to sit on. I had a blanket to fold and sit on or pull over me. There was no windshield so we had to go slow and it was 11:30 p.m. before we got to Chatham, more dead than alive. I was completely stiff from sitting on that board for ten hours. I was also frozen from the cold. I got my blood circulating again and helped the mechanic fix the car, before we both went to sleep for a couple of hours in the barn, in a pile of hay. The next day, it was raining, and I shined the car up before going home to rest.

When I had my picture taken for my chauffeur's license, I had some extras, so I am sending you one. I had four pictures and they cost me $1.50 that is considerably more than it would cost in Copenhagen. I expect a stop in the mail now until I get to Bermuda. It will take two weeks longer for the mail to get there. If you put on the envelope - VIA HALIFAX, CANADA - they will get there faster as that is where the ship starts from and the Danish ships, also stop there most of the time before going to New York.

The best to all, Hal

Chatham, New York
Dec. 4, 1916

Now our Bermuda trip is set for Dec. 20, so we will be there for Christmas. We will leave Chatham on Dec.18 and New York Dec. 20 and be in Bermuda Dec. 22 and now I hope it is right this time.

I have got some information about Mr. Payn. He is from Ghent, where he went to school as a very poor boy without shoes and in ragged dirty clothes. He was always crazy about horses and grew up to be a racehorse driver on the racetracks and even now, he can handle four horses pulling a wagon, although he is now 82 years old and he can do it better than anyone else around here. He has about 40 horses around on different farms he owns, mostly racehorses. No one here knows how he got his first money, but he got into politics and is a high ranking Republican. One day an oil company in Pennsylvania went broke and he took over the company lock, stock and barrel, oil wells and all. At the time, the automobile was just beginning to be used and he raised the money to remodel the whole works. He got to be a State Insurance Commissioner and built his house in Chatham where he now lives and he built and operates the Payn Boxboard Mills and also, the Chatham Bank. Now he is a millionaire several times over. His wife is much younger and her people are from Kinderhook. It is said that she was his secretary in his office as Insurance Commissioner in Albany and is his second wife. Her name was Heath. He has children with his first wife, but his son is living in New York and I have heard that he drinks too much and the old man is very much against that. I have never heard about his son working and no one knows anything about the daughter he is suppose to have out west somewhere.

I don't expect much out of Christmas this year as I will be in a climate, that doesn't give you much impression of a Danes idea of Christmas with Santa Claus, snowmen and elves, but I can go swimming in the ocean and pick strawberries and flowers. I know I will miss you all and even if I say to myself others are in the same boat, it don't help much. I remember when I was fourteen years old and went to Jersey and worked in the grocery store there. That was not as far away as here, but I was real sad and down in the dumps then, for being away from home.

The best to all, Hal

Chatham
Dec. 12, 1916

Dearest all,

Now it must be something I can believe for the tickets arrived and Mr. and Mrs. Payn are leaving Chatham Sunday Dec. 17 and the Bermuda ship, a steamer, is leaving New York Dec. 20th., so it will be a Christmas trip. It takes two days (48 hours) to get there from New York and it is a rough trip down the Gulf Stream and usually many people are seasick, so I have something to look forward to. Even with no wind, the ship will roll and tumble around in the waves, but I hope for the best. I don't know if Mr. and Mrs. Payn will have me drive them down to New York, but I doubt that, as it will be a slow and cold trip in this cold weather so I suppose they will take a train. But the car is going to New York and stay at the factory all winter for an overhaul to be ready to go next spring. It can be a rough trip, as it is now snowing. It started last night and it has snowed all night and all day, but it is not very cold and completely calm so the roads are still open. The snow is sticking to the trees and filling the branches so they are all white and cloaked in snow. It is a beautiful sight and I like seeing a little winter before I leave and move into the summer again, but I keep my fingers crossed and hope I can drive to New York City.

I have had no letters from you in three weeks so I think there is mail for me in Bermuda. I am told in January they have some cold days and need a little heat there. Then they use kerosene ovens. They are really poor there, have no stoves and kerosene and must freeze. The rain showers are sudden and a lot of water falls from the sky in a short time. The clouds start to form overhead in a clear sky and they then spread out and before you know it and have time to get inside, you are soaked. When you get this, your Christmas is over, but I will think of you all on Christmas eve. I have my shoes to the shoemaker, he charged one dollar to straighten the heel and put new soles on.

Merry Christmas to all, Love Hal

Chatham, New York
Dec. 17, 1916

This is my last night here in Chatham. It is Sunday evening and I am here in the house all alone. I took a bath and I am now sitting in the dining room writing on the dining table. It is 7:27 p.m. Mr. And Mrs. Stupplebeen and also Elizabeth drove to Ghent about 2-3 miles from here. They have a horse and used a sled to get there, every time a sled goes by on the street you can hear the bells ringing. It is a nice sound. No cars are going by. I guess no one wants to try to drive in the snow. There were two other men staying here, but they left for the holidays and tomorrow I leave. We have got more snow since my last letter, but not as much as in New York City. In the paper, they said one foot fell there yesterday, so I can expect a difficult trip there tomorrow if there are drifts, but Mr. Stupplebeen is going with me.

I was out with the car this morning to try the road and it was so bad I got stuck and had to get a farmer to come out with a team of horses to pull me out of the drift. There is no snow removal from the roads and where I got stuck, there was three feet of snow for a distance of 150 feet where it had drifted in. The roads are good now for horse and sled and you see a lot of them. Mr. and Mrs. Payn left for New York City yesterday and I will not see them before we get on the ship. The coachman and stable boy go to New York tomorrow evening with a freight train and bring the three horses with them that go on the ship with us to Bermuda. They have hired another man to stay here in Chatham to look after the horses that are staying here. I got my ticket to Bermuda on the Quebec steamship Company's Bermuda Line. The ship's name is "The Bermudian". It cost $50.00 round trip and comes from Canada, stays in New York and leaves again for Bermuda Wednesday, Dec. 20 at 11:00 a.m. I have made a discovery. In Denmark, I saw a moving picture called "Neptune's Daughter" and I remember the beautiful scenery in the film. Now I hear it was filmed in Bermuda and was shown there last winter. If you get a chance to see it you will like it and know a little bit more about this island that I now soon will see. The water there is crystal clear and has a blue tint in the distance. The ground is either sandy, but mostly red or rust colored. There is only a thin layer of dirt on top of the rocks that show through. The rocks are white, but turn gray when exposed to the sun and air and are all coral, that look like sandstone. They are never more than five to ten feet under the water. This rock can be sawed with an ordinary saw and in a quarry are sawed into blocks and are used for building houses, paving the roads, or as roof covering. It can not be exported to New York because it crumbles when it freezes. There is no water on the island and everywhere are cisterns for collecting rainwater as that is the only fresh water there. The roofs on the houses are whitewashed once a year and are used to collect rainwater that runs into a cistern under every house.

I see in the paper that Buffalo Bill is dead. I saw him in the circus in Copenhagen doing trick shooting and riding. He had started his circus and traveled with it all over America and Europe after he quit his job for the government as an Indian fighter and guide. The only thing I can send you for Christmas is this handkerchief enclosed. I sent one in my last letter. At least it is something from here. The information on Bermuda, I got from the coachman, he has been there several times. I am going to be a gardener when I get there.

Good luck and Merry Christmas to you all.

Hal.

New York
Dec. 19, 1916

I am now in New York; we arrived here about 5 p.m. after a fairly good trip from Chatham and more or less fighting snowdrifts on the way down. But it was not too bad, and I never had to use the shovel, I brought along. The snow had been on the ground a couple of days and was packed down by the traffic. I just followed the ruts and sometimes they were frozen so I couldn't get out of them once in them. We got here safe and sound. We left Chatham at 8 a.m. and Mr. Stupplebeen and I had our lunch in Poughkeepsie where we stopped for forty minutes. The speedometer showed 139 miles today, I have been around to get my passport as I just found out I will need one to go to Bermuda because it is an English Island.

First, I went to the Danish Consul to get a Danish passport, I was lucky, I had my birth certificate with me, so I had no trouble with that. Then, I had to go to the British Consulate for a visa and the first thing they said was "You look like a German to me". I had to give them my name, address, birthplace and that was all on my passport. Then they wanted to know how long I was here and where I worked and why I was going to Bermuda. I finally got the visa, but they told me, I could not be sure they would let me in there. That was up to the local people and if they thought, I was German; I would have to come back. Then I had to go to the State Auto Bureau to get my chauffeur's license renewed as they all run out on New Years Day. That cost me two dollars so now I was ready to go. It took me all day, but tomorrow we are off to Bermuda and I am ready for my seasick trip. I have to expect that. We are all on 1st class and will have the run of the whole ship and excellent food if you can eat it.

I have not seen Frank, the coachman, but Mr. Stupplebeen was going to help him get aboard with the horses. Frank says "No seasick for me, I am there every time for the eats". I will now leave the car at the factory and then go to the hotel and to bed for my last night here.

Love to all. Hal

CHAPTER SIX

Off to Bermuda

December 24, 1916
Sunday A.M. "Paynhurst"

I will have to write this morning, so I can get this letter in the mail today. Then it will leave with "The Bermudian" tomorrow. We had a rough trip here and I was seasick most of the time. We took three days to get here instead of the usual two days on account of the stormy weather. It was a nasty snowstorm when we left New York. When I got up out of bed on the 3rd day, Saturday morning, we were in calm water in a bay outside Hamilton. It was the nicest summer weather you could wish for. That was quite a change from New York and I enjoyed it. After breakfast, the ship started to move slowly up the bay and into the harbor, but it was Saturday afternoon before we got off the ship. The men wore straw hats and the women had light colored summer dresses on. Some wore parasols for the sun. It was beautiful here and flowers were everywhere. The nights here are also mild but damp and the dew starts falling when the sun goes down. If you turn your face up you can feel it like a dust falling on you from a clear sky. There was one letter for me mailed Nov. 7 so that took about six weeks to get here. It had been here one week with the last ship. I may get more letters with this ship, but that will take three days as all the mail has to be censored.

We had a bad experience on the ship coming here. A lot of old and sick people were on the ship. There was this one man traveling with his nurse and his wife and four children. I was told he was going to Bermuda to rest after a nervous breakdown. One night he jumped overboard, and the ship stopped, but in the stormy sea they could not find him, so he is still out there.

"PAYNHURST" Payn's Bermuda Estate

We finally arrived at Paynhurst. Everything is a mess here and we can't find anything yet, but we are slowly getting settled. We came here Saturday afternoon and it took us the rest of the day to get everything up to the estate (Paynhurst). It is a big house on top of a cliff. The road goes through an iron gate up the side of the cliff and comes out on top, goes by the house that has a tower at one end. It also has a staircase and a flat roof from where we can see all over the Islands.

The road runs through the garden and to the stables where we put the three horses and our rooms are over the stable. When we finally got somewhat settled we were hungry and then we realized we had nothing to eat and all the stores were closed. We had some candy we ate and the next day we tried to buy something, but it was Sunday and we still couldn't get anything. Tonight is Christmas Eve so tomorrow evening is also closed being Christmas Day. This place is across the bay from Hamilton and there is a ferry going about every hour so I went to town and had a cup of tea and some cookies in a place. I found a teahouse. I see a lot of niggers here and also the Portuguese farmers and they are all out to swindle the tourists as they know most tourists don't understand the money here. It is very hard to figure out the mixture of American and English money. You can pay in either one and get change in both kinds of money mixed together so you don't know what you are getting.

The only white girl here at Payn's is an Irish girl who works in the house. Mrs. Payn brought her down here with her. Then there is a black cook from Jamaica and another girl that helps in the house, she is also colored black and is a Bermudian, then there is a gardener-caretaker that lives nearby. He is Portuguese and his name is Frith. He looks after the estate when Mr. Payn is away as he lives here all year around.

The white Irish girl Marie told me she was here last year and she knows the girls on the next estate and they were all going to midnight church in the cathedral in Hamilton this being Christmas Eve. So I went with her and we were joined by some girls from the other place and two other men. I went to church and it was nice with candles and Christmas Carols. It was 2:30 a.m. on Monday, Dec. 25th when we got out. The air was a bit cool, but I had no overcoat on and after we got walking we were all right. I was glad to meet the people from this other place. It is a very wealthy family that lives there. They have a big yacht tied up along the house and the people I met were the servants. These people worked in two shifts and had a separate building where they lived. They had their own cook and dining room. They had their own servants waiting on them in the dining room and girls to clean their rooms and a laundry where all the wash was taken care of.

The letter I got from you had some pictures also from Solveig, pictures of Grandmother. I will write more when I get a chance.

The best to all

Hal

December 25 1916
Monday

Dearest

This is Christmas day and we still have had nothing to eat to speak of, so Frank went to the kitchen and talked to the black cook and she gave us enough for a lunch this noon. I helped Frank with the horses. He then went to the City and picked up the mail and there was a letter for me. I have no feeling of Christmas this year, but we will have our own celebration tomorrow after our shopping spree. I have not yet been any place on this Island except to town at night and around the place here. Frith, the caretaker, has been taking care of the vegetable garden here. We have new potatoes, radishes and onions. Also flowers, mostly Lilies which are raised on most farms here with onions for export and then sweet potatoes. Most trees are Cedar, small trees, along the road coming up to the entrance. Paynhurst - the big house is near the edge of a cliff and the road going down to the highway, which is fairly narrow as no cars are allowed here and all transportation is by horse or wagon.

There are no lakes, rivers, creeks, ponds or wells. The only water is rainwater from the roofs running down into cisterns. The water is clear and clean, but always lukewarm and you can't get a cold glass of water unless you put ice in it. The sun is not out today and it is a little cold as the wind is strong and we have had a couple of rain showers. It is warm enough inside without heat and I have the windows open so I can smell the clean fresh ocean air. I have to get this in the mail today so it will be on the ship leaving tomorrow. I will write again soon.

The best to all

Hal

**Later on Christmas
December 25, 8 p.m.**

It is now Christmas today, our time is different from yours about 5 hours later so now at 8 p.m. is already 1 a.m. Tuesday in Copenhagen and I am thinking of you and hope you have had a nice Christmas. I know you started Christmas Eve with rice pudding and fried chicken as there is no goose to be had now while the war is going on. I surely hope the United States don't get into that conflict, and Denmark neither. I am sitting here by a table with a stable lantern for light while I am writing. I got a full meal tonight, but I don't know what it was. The trouble for me here is there are only two kinds of restaurants, no lunchrooms where you can get a good meal for a low price. The people here are either tourists or Portuguese and Negroes. The restaurants for Tourists are good, but I can't afford their prices, 5 to 10 dollars for a meal in the hotel, and the food in the other places are not for white people and you see only Negroes in them. The white don't mix much with the Negroes here any more than they do in the states. No American would sit down and eat with a Negro and I think that is wrong. The Negroes are as good as some whites I know and I never could understand people would show such an attitude, but that is the way it is and it is already beginning to rub off on me, because I know other whites would consider me a low class no good if they saw me associate with Negroes. For the time being, I will eat and work with

Frank and he is a good man and I also like the Portuguese caretaker Frith.

The Negroes here cannot own any property, no house and no farms, where the Portuguese can. We finished our work by 5 p.m. - the horses were fed and everything was swept and cleaned so I sort of expected Mrs. Payn to invite us up to the house for a Christmas dinner. We didn't see Mr. and Mrs. Payn all day and now we were finished with our work and had no food, so Frank said he knew of a place about 5 minutes walk from "Paynhurst" where we could possibly get something to eat. We walked over there and it was a Negro hut. A small room with two tables and chairs, but it looked clean and a young nigger girl came and put out a white tablecloth on one table that had a white covering so I think it was because of us, or maybe me a white man, that we got the extra services. It didn't look like a real restaurant because they were also selling soft drinks and candy and Negroes were coming in and buying things and leaving again and they all knew one another and they even introduced me to some of the young Negro girls and fellows so it was more like being in a private home. Some of them had seen me before and known me as Mr. Payn's new chauffeur. I think some of them worked in the white peoples' houses as servants. Everybody was happy and laughing and we soon got served a meal. They put some white bread on the table, also sugar, cream and mustard and then a cup of tea. The bread was not wheat. I think they had some meat in it. Then we got a platter of food, it had a slice of ham on it and then a hot pie, but it was like no pie I have had in the states. It was a specialty they make for Christmas. It had several kinds of meat in it. Some chicken, ham, pork, beef and others I don't know. It may have been goat meat as you see a lot of goats all over. I don't know what they used for dough to keep it together and the gravy was a mystery, but we were hungry and it tasted so good we ate it all up. We were full and got up to pay. The girl said "One and six" for each. I didn't know what she was talking about, but it turned out to be 1 shilling and 6 pence. One shilling is like a quarter and 6 pence is 1/2 quarter as it takes 12 pence for a shilling. I think it was a high price, but this is a tourist land and much food and sometimes even water has to be shipped here from the states. I can buy a meal in a lunchroom in New York City for 25 cents and get soup, meat with potatoes and pie and coffee, 1 1/2 shilling was high, but it was fun to have Christmas Dinner with the natives. The girl waiting on the table wished us a Merry Christmas and hoped we would come again, so I went home and started this letter. Frank went with his Negro friends to Hamilton where a Negro orchestra is playing in the square.

All last night we could hear music. The Negroes play horns and sing, they go from house to house and I could hear one word it was "Gloria" it was a Christmas song. Many Negroes are really nice people and good workers, but they are mostly used as servants, waiters and laborers. The farmers here are mostly descendants from Portuguese sailors as no Negroes can own land or any other real estate on this Island and you can not vote unless you own property here. We have kerosene stove here for our cooking and heating and spent several hours cleaning some rusty skillets that have not been used since last winter. Then Frank went up to the house and came back with a white tablecloth he got from one of the girls. It is going to be sort of primitive here, but we can think of it as camping.

I have been to Hamilton to buy supplies and I also got 34 picture postcards I am going to start sending here and there and you will get most of them. We take a little ferry boat across the bay to Hamilton, if we take the road around the bay it is 2 1/2 miles, but only 1/2 mile with the ferry. The money here is giving me trouble. What do you think of a bill like this? I got it after buying a few things for our housekeeping.

....	8
....	2/3
....	10
....	4
....	11
Total	5 shillings

Lis Clark

That was 5 shillings I paid for it, but I don't understand it yet. You write that Soren wants to go in the automobile business and sell cars if he can get an agency. He better get some money together first, that is what it takes.

Love to all

Hal

December 28, 1916
Paynhurst

The only white girl working here for Mrs. Payn is the little Irish girl Marie. She asked me to go with her to Hamilton as we are the only two white people working here, so we sort of talk and shop together and she can help me with the money as she has been here before. I will now introduce all the people living here at "Paynhurst". There are Mr. and Mrs. Payn and Mrs. Payn's sister Miss Margaret Heed, then Mrs. Payn's mother Mrs. Heed. Then there is Mr. Hues who has a small factory in Malden Bridge, New York where he makes wooden water pumps for farmers' wells. He is an old friend of Mr. Payn and visits with them a lot in Chatham and is going to be here for a few weeks. In the house is Marie, the Irish girl (white), Mary, the cook (black). Fanny (also black) helps cleaning in the house. Then there are Frith, the Portuguese descent caretaker and gardener, also Frank the coachman (Negro) and finally myself. Mr. Hues is a nice man about 55-60 years old and I think Mrs. Payn likes him to be here to be Mr. Payn's companion. Sometimes, Mr. Payn's son is here for a few days they tell me, but I didn't see him yet. This is a short letter, but the mail must go now so a happy New Year to all.

Hal

FRANK the coachman

FRITH the caretaker

Marie the housemaid

<u>*FANNY*</u> *the house cleaner*

Jan. 11, 1917

Dear all

Hurray - I got all my Christmas mail and newspaper Monday, so now I have something to read. Thanks for everything. It has taken 2 months to get here. The steamer "Bermudian" comes again every Friday and returns to Canada on Sunday so now I expect to get letters every Monday. Now after New Years it is really starting to get cold in the States so the season begins here and the tourists are coming. The biggest hotel in Hamilton, the "Hotel Hamilton" opened with eight guests last week, but this week a bunch of guests arrived and more are expected every week. Business is slow this year on account of the war in Europe. I hope the US doesn't get involved. I see in the papers that Denmark is in the process of planning a vote on selling the Virgin Islands to the US, and that you have shortages of most things like chickens, eggs and onions, but there are no shortages here.

I am sorry to hear that your neighbor, my Godmother, died at the party in town, so I will not see her when I get back - or several other people who have passed away since I left.

It is a shame to sell the Virgin Islands, but I suppose little Denmark needs the money now, and the US has it, Thanks to Solveig, I got pictures from home and I enjoy that. Now I have bought a little camera, a Brownie, so I can have a record of my trip - who knows, I may never get here again, so a camera is the best way to help remember. I will send copies to Solveig.

The white girl here, Marie, also has a camera - so have the cook, Mary, and also the other black girl, Fanny. I have taken pictures of Mrs. Payn's house and garden and I will mail the results as soon as I can. So far, I have been helping Frank, the coachman, to get everything cleaned and the three horses have been washed, polished and cleaned so they are shining, and so are the wagons and other gear. So, we have been working hard, but now everything is in order and we can take it a little easy, and there is really no more work than Frank can do himself. Mr. Payn knows that and he came out to talk to me one day, and told me he had some work for me in the garden, so to let Frank do his own work.

Now I am helping the gardener, Frith. He is a Bermudian, but I think he is half Indian. He is white, but has a broad nose like the Negroes, and a thin mouth like a white man, but black stiff hair like an Indian. He is an unusually nice person and after Mr. Payn told me what he wanted done, I told him, and we then worked together.

Now I will have more time to get out as I don't have to do chores morning and night, and I can take off on Sundays all day. Frank told me he never has had a whole day off in the three years he has worked for Mr. Payn, so I told him I would do his work some Sunday so he could get off, and he liked that.

The girl Marie had last Sunday off and she and I went to the neighbors and asked the help there what they had planned for the day, so we all went together and rented a sailboat and the fisherman that owned it. He took us on a trip to Sommerset, a little town on the other end of the Island. We went ashore there and had lunch in a little inn, and the owner showed us a room where the King of England, King George, stayed and slept in the bed 27 years ago. We walked around a little and up a hill, looked over the water and landscape, and then went back to the sailboat. It was mid-afternoon, but the wind had died down and it took a long time to get back. The sun went down and the moon came up, and it was a beautiful trip, but it was expensive - it cost me $3.00 - so I am not able to do that every Sunday; but here you can go all over on bicycles, and that is easy. I found out Marie can't ride a bicycle - she never has - so she is going to be a drag on me, as she is always trying to go with me, and always asks me to go to Hamilton with her. Maybe, I can teach her to ride.

The Island is 25 miles long and 3 miles broad at the widest part. Bermuda is a lot of Islands, and it is claimed that there are 365 Islands.

Some only a couple of acres, most 5-10 acres, and others up to 50 acres. But the main Island is, as I said, 3 miles by 25 miles, and has roads on it, but only for horses and wagons - no cars. I will send you a map of the Islands.

Mr. and Mrs. Payn's friend Mr. Hues has been a farmer and he got Mr. Payn to buy a cow that gave milk, so that they could have fresh milk. He is the only one who knows how to milk, so he comes down to the stables twice a day in his good clothes, takes off his jacket and milks the cow while the whole gang stands watching. When he is done, he puts his jacket on again and carries the milk up to the kitchen. Now I have the job of putting the cow out on the lawn and tie her and feed her. This is a very important job for the time being, so I got it.

Hal

Jan, 17, 1917
Paynhurst, Bermuda

No letters for me this week, so better luck next boat. Everything is going smoothly - I help Frank to feed the horses in the morning and put the cow out where I can find some grass for her. I had my suit to the tailor to be cleaned and pressed. He was black; so was the barber that cut my hair. We buy our food in a store run by a Negro.

I like the little ferryboat, the South Kettle Ferry, bringing us back and forth to Hamilton. The traffic is confusing as the British drive on the left and you see a lot of people on bicycles. The weather has been quite changeable, one day warm and nice, and the next day cold and always windy like it is in Denmark in the summertime. I have taken some pictures around here, and hope they turn out good. Too bad you can't get them in color - that would really show what it is like here, but the photographer here in Hamilton colors pictures by hand and he is good at it and I suppose it is expensive.

The temperature tonight is down to 64 degrees., and with the wind here it is cold. I didn't get this letter off in time, so I am adding to it here.

Later
Jan. 23, 1917

I will have to tell you about an experience I had yesterday - there was an earthquake here. They get them, but seldom. The last was 3 years ago; here is the way it was :

I was sitting in my room waiting my supper at 6:30 p.m., and the weather was perfect. All of my windows were open, and then I heard a sound like a strong wind going through the tree-tops. I could see the trees swaying and the sound was coming closer, and suddenly it was all around me before I had time to get up and close the windows. I couldn't understand the wind coming on suddenly, but now the building started to shake like an Express Train went by, and the glass started to move in the windows frames like they were going to fall out. Suddenly it was over, and everything was quiet. Now I could hear the dogs barking all around. I had grabbed hold of the chair I was sitting on and it had slid along the floor. The dogs were still barking and I now realized it was an earthquake because the wind could not have done that. There was no wind, so I got up and ran down the stairs and outside. I was thinking it could start again in a few minutes and I wanted to be sure I didn't get the roof down over my head. When I got out everything was quiet, and the dogs had stopped barking.

It was a warm nice evening, but there were now tree branches on the lawn. I could now hear the birds sing and twitter and some natives blowing horns and singing some distance away. I thought the danger was over and I went upstairs and finished my supper.

It was over and nothing more happened - no serious damage. Next day, I talked to Frith about it and he said it happens here, but the last time was 3 years ago, and they never had any damage from an earthquake. The Island is a big coral rock and someone once tried to drill down to see if they could find water; they drilled through the rock 3000 feet and then found a sandy ocean bottom, so the Island is really a big rock just laying in the ocean on the bottom and reaching over the surface over the water.

Last Saturday I went to Hamilton after supper and I saw the Salvation Army Band - about 20 Negroes playing and singing. They drew a big crowd and after each number, lasting about 10 minutes, a man would talk and then they would play again. It was nice and people enjoyed it. There is quite a bunch of tourists here now, but not as many as were expected; the War is spreading and people are afraid to sail here, afraid of the German submarines.

Sunday afternoon I took a walk with Frith down to "South Shore Beach", about 20 minutes walk right across the island to the ocean. It was a nice warm day and I had to take my jacket off - it was too warm. It was a beautiful beach. Some people were bathing; the sand was clean and white. At each end of the beach the rocks go right out in the ocean and sort of enclose the beach. It is about 1/2 mile long. I took some pictures I am sending you. A big hotel is built right on the beach, and some of the guests were horseback riding on the beach. About one mile out in the ocean a big freighter had run aground about 2 years ago. The front part was fast on the rocks, and the other end was broken off and had sunk in the ocean. You could rent boats and someone would row you out to the ship, you can get aboard it and go exploring inside. The seamen on the rear part of the ship all died when the ship broke in two, but the men on the front part were saved. The water here is clear, salt, and calm - it looks a nice blue from little ways out to as far as you can see. Sometimes it is green in close, and you can see the ocean bottom in deep water. There are plenty of sharks in the water, but they don't get in here as this beach is protected by a rock ring going from one end of the beach in a circle out where the wreck is and up to the other end of the beach. The sharks stay outside in deep water and have never come in to shore.

You can go out in a boat and fish for sharks, and last winter someone hooked 2 sharks. They took them to the hotel kitchen where they were prepared and served to the guests, but they are not easy to land and have to be killed by chopping their heads off with an ax. They have a mouth big enough to get a man's head in it and very sharp teeth. Frith and I walked home and planned to go fishing sometime.

The cedars that grow over most of the island are small, but other trees are very tall. Here are no apple or pear trees, but you see orange trees and palms. The farmers can get potatoes - three crops a year - you only see new red potatoes and sweet potatoes. Apples brought down here are expensive and will not keep very long. You see banana trees - they have a stalk of bananas and then die as a new stalk grows up from the roots. I have also seen sugar plants. They look something like corn and a few people have them. You can buy a length of sugar stalk in the store and the natives buy it and chew on it to get the sugar.

I am sorry to hear you have to use stamps for buying sugar and meat and milk and butter and many other things. Here Frank and I use about 20 dollars per month for both of us for food, but we have to buy mostly canned goods as things don't keep good in this climate. We get enough to eat, but keep to things we can make easily on the little stove.

Hope you are all well - more soon.

Hal

Jan. 31, 1917

Dear all

I received some letters from you mailed on Dec. 7 and Dec. 15, with some pictures. I will send you a few pictures from my sail trip to "Sommerset". Last Sunday we went to St. George at the other end of the Island. This main Island is 25 miles long, and Hamilton is about midway between. Paynhurst is also in the middle and we have 14 miles to St. George. I will send you a map.

This is a coral island built up of tiny living animals and the white coral is the housing they build for themselves. I get my information from the photographer in Hamilton who does my work.

He likes to talk with me, and I understand him good. He is a Hungarian and he has been here a long time. He said this Island was under water when the little coral animals built it up over the last million years, and then the bottom of the ocean raised and the Island with it. He also knew of a time when no rain fell to speak of for 18 months and most of the people here fled from the Islands. Drilling for water has not produced any as they can find only salt water; at more than 3000 feet they find old ocean bottom and sand, but no fresh water. The north end of the Island continues under water out for about 10 miles and that place is two small rocks that reach over the surface of the ocean and a lighthouse is now built there. They cut a canal through this rock formation and made it possible for ships to go through into calm water.

They found roots of cedar wood to show this land was once above water but has now again sunk below the ocean surface. With glass bottom boats you can go out and see the fish and coral formation living there; also swamp and ferns growing in splendid colors.

On Bermuda you will find caves and water filled holes claimed to have no bottom. They have salt water and fall and rise with the tide in the ocean. Of course, a tunnel-like connection goes down and continues on to the ocean miles away, and that explains the fact that the natives insist there is no bottom.

That is all...

The best to you all

Hal

Lis Clark

Feb. 7, 1917
Bermuda

Dear Mom and Dad

Thanks for the letter of Jan. 10. That is fast and I just got it, but some of my mail you sent around Christmastime is not here yet. I am feeling fine and I have been cutting and trimming trees. Mrs. Payn and I took a walk around the garden the other day and she wanted some low spots in the lawn filled up level and then she said that she was going to get me three or four niggers to help me and I could look after them and tell them how to do it. We then got over to where the big trees lined the edge of the cliff - actually it is more like a bank, as you can walk down it hanging on to the shrubbery - and I said if the trees were trimmed some she would have a better view from her windows over the bay and harbor. She thought it was a good idea and we could do that too.

We got going on the job with the lawn. Frith got a dumpcart pulled by a jackass and he got two niggers to dig some dirt up in the far back of the garden and put it in the cart. He took it up to me on the lawn where I and two niggers spread it and got it leveled, so that worked out good except for the back lot where the dirt was scraped clear to the rocks about a foot down.

Then I put the niggers to work weeding the rose bed and Frith sowed grass seed in the new dirt in the lawn. We worked at that one week and then I tackled the trees. It turned out that the longest ladder we could get was, with extension, 32 feet, and not long enough to reach the top of the trees. On top of that none of the niggers wanted to climb up that high, so I had to do it. I didn't mind, so I sawed the limbs off and the niggers and Frith, with the jackass and dump wagon cut it up and took it away. Everything worked out very good and now Mrs. Payn also wanted a few trees cut down and the roots dug up, so that will keep us all busy for another couple of weeks.

Mrs. Payn got a couple of coral stone blocks and was going to try to carry them out for a birdbath - stone is so soft so you can cut it with a knife and hammer and chisel or saw - so she has been working on that and it is starting to look like a birdbath now. She told me she was getting afraid to go back to the States as the Germans have been sinking so many English ships and they may come over on this side of the ocean. The ship that comes here, "The Bermudian" is British and it could be torpedoed.   Well, we can do nothing about that, and I am sure I want to go back come Spring. It is nice here in winter to get away from the cold, but I would sure not like to stay until the War is over. So, if I can get a ship, I will be going back to USA.

I am still thinking, I would like to go to Detroit or out West in order to see as much as possible of this big country while I am here, so we will see what develops. I so enjoy getting all those pictures that Solveig is sending and it is sort of lonesome here as I am always either working, sleeping or writing letters. But I suppose I am doing this work here because I want to do it or I wouldn't be here. I wish I could just talk to you all for a while. I am getting tired of living with Negroes, I guess. I am getting better at talking and understanding English. I understand you are suffering somewhat with all the restrictions now on account of the War. I am glad that we don't have that here.

I hope you all get enough to eat. We eat good enough, but I can't buy Margarine - they don't have it, but butter costs 50c a pound. I just came from the store and I had to pay two shillings for it. Eggs are 3 shillings (75c) a dozen. Sugar is 4 1/2 penny (9c) and smoked ham 27c per pound, sliced. We buy mostly thing in cans - they keep better for us and a lot of things can only be had that way here, like tobacco in cans. The damp weather spoils things fast like smoked, salted meat in cans - when they are opened they only last a few days, then they get moldy. We can also buy Norwegian sardines in cans for 27c. We buy milk in cans and smoked salmon, headcheese and sometimes butter -

all in cans. The store is half full of shelving with cans. It is good for us, as we can keep it longer. We drink mostly tea.

We have had cold or cool weather for about one week now, and some rain, and I am hoping for some better weather soon. I am waiting for your letters and hope Dad is better and over his cold. Here the natives gargle with kerosene for a sore throat and cold.

I am getting to be an expert on climbing trees and from the tops I can see all over the city and the bay.

The best to all,

Hal

Feb. 22, 1917
Paynhurst

Dear all

I had a postcard from you this week and I am sorry to hear Dad is still in bed with his cold - that has lasted too long now, so I wish he could get here and enjoy some warmer weather. We don't get the weather we are suppose to get, although it is much better than New York. All last week was cold, but Sunday and Monday it was warm summer, then Tuesday rain and wind. But they claim next month will be much better. Last Sunday I woke up to this nice summer weather, it was warm and the wind was down. I could hear the roosters crow, as most all natives have poultry and dogs. I lay there in bed and felt real good. And, I somehow imagined I was home in my own bed, and the roosters crowing were from Aders Benton's farm up the road from our school. Then, I said to myself when I really woke up "You are out of your head, you are in Bermuda. It is winter in Denmark and you are 3500 miles away from home and I miss you all".

Marie, the only white girl working here for Mrs. Payn had that day off and in that nice weather we and the crowd from next door went down to the beach in the afternoon to go swimming. We were seven of us. I took some pictures I will send to you soon.

The garden here is doing well and we now have strawberries, a lot of them. Who would ever think I would be eating strawberries in the month of February? You just think real hard about it and I will bet you can almost taste them, they are so good. What? -You are not giving up so soon, just sit down and eat some more. I am sure you can eat a few more - here are more of them.

The other day I bought a piece of sugar cane in the store. It was two yards long and I tried to chew it, the pulp inside is very sweet and the kids like to get them, but I was soon finished. I went to the picture show last night and saw "Neptune's Daughter" - and it was photographed here a couple of years ago and shows some of the scenery and the water filled caves.

The best to all,

Hal

March 19, 1917
Paynhurst, Bermuda

I got your letters from February 11 last night and I needed them as I didn't get any last week and this is now 3 weeks since my last letter to you. So Dad has been to the doctor and had something done to his ears and nose - that must be sinus he has, and I hope he is well again, now.

I am sending some pictures from my bicycle trip to St. George on the other end of the Islands and from other beautiful spots along the way. Now, while I think about it, you better start sending my letters to Chatham again, because I expect to be there around May 1st.

I lost my travel companion, Marie. She went back to New York, she said she quit her job because she didn't' want to work here for these people anymore. She said the girls were overworked and most of the time didn't get enough food to eat.

I was down to the next estate and we had a little party there. There is one man I especially like. His name is George and he is the butler on the estate and also butler on the yacht when they are sailing. He has been most places in Europe, mostly in the Mediterranean countries, but also to Denmark one time, and he was in Tivoli. We were eating sandwiches and cake and drinking Ginger Beer. They played the gramophone and danced. Before leaving we had tea and cake. You can see these people on the pictures I am sending here from the day we were down to the beach. The weather is now much better, but we will have to think about leaving soon, as spring is here. We still get strawberries, also a fruit called Paw-Paw from Paw-Paw trees, I didn't like them. They have to be peeled and the insides scraped out like you would a melon. Bananas are plentiful and cost seven cents a pound. I eat them and a lot of eggs. We also have oranges here, but they are small.

There is no Lutheran church here, but most all other denominations. The natives go to church every Sunday and the churches are always full. It must be getting close to Easter as the stores are full of candy Easter eggs.

I can now read the headlines in the newspapers and they mention Denmark and the Virgin Islands. I am wondering if the sale has gone through and Denmark lost the Islands. I will have to get a newspaper and try to read it.

Eggs are going down in price every week and we eat more of them. Now we get gingerbread and bologna. Frank usually takes Mr. and Mrs. Payn and guests, if any, for a small trip every afternoon, usually to Hamilton. The horses have to be exercised and every forenoon the Payn's take a walk around the garden and say "good morning" to me and Frank, then they say something about the weather or the work. If Frank mentions we need something for the horses they will say "already again?" so they must be tight with all their money. The girls in the house told me for a dinner for eight people they only had 2 small chickens and only one leg came back from the table for the 3 girls to eat, so they are always complaining. Marie left, but they got a Negro girl to take her place.

The best to all

Hal.

March 27, 1917
Paynhurst

Today I received a letter sent from Denmark on Jan. 29, and I am glad to hear you are all well again. The vote for town leaders is coming up and I am wondering if Dad is again taking the job as supervisor and get all the work of keeping the books. They pay you a little for it, but it is hardly worth it to take the job for $50 a year if you are not feeling too good. I am waiting to hear more about the Virgin Islands - it must have been in the papers here, but right now they are full of War, and more War.

You write about Negroes in the Virgin Islands making trouble and striking, but everything is quiet here in Bermuda, so I can't understand why they would make trouble for Denmark so they would have to send a Destroyer there. Do they want to belong to the USA? Here any Bermudian that wants to leave can do so and go to USA and many do for the summer, and then come back here for the winter tourist season.

People of different colors keep to their own and the government provides separate schools here as is done in the States. The churches are mostly also segregated, but if a Negro wants to go to a white church nobody says anything, and they are welcome, but as a general rule everyone wants to go to their own. I can understand that as I know if there were a Danish Lutheran Church here I would be there too - I guess everybody feels more comfortable with their own color and nationality. In Hamilton there are two churches built one against the other. One is for white, the other for black, and down the street is another church for mulattos and Portuguese. People go where they want to go - it is a free country as to that. The Negroes will greet whites if you meet them on the road and they will say "Good Morning" up till 12 noon, after that they say "Good Afternoon", and after 6 p.m. they will say "Good Night", not good evening as we say in the States.

I am told the Islands were discovered around the year 1650 and a few English settlers came here later, and descendants from their own land are the ruling white class. For a couple of hundreds years, pirates used the Islands and the rumor was spread that Devils and evil spirits lived here, and the Islands were shunned by seamen, as storms wrecked their ships and the ones that tried to get here never returned. The storms and rough water are still here, and plenty of wrecks lie under the ocean around this Island that is surrounded by the warm waters of the Gulf Stream. The Gulf is a rough and tough road to sail and the warm water is rolling the ships, and causes storms. Now, with better ships, it is no problem to get here, and the underwater coral reefs are marked so ships can sail safely here. The Island is ringed by a coral reef, but the government has cut canals through the reef so that ships can sail into the city of Hamilton.

The Island of St. George is the second in size here, and got its name from a Captain George. The Islands were then supposedly full of devils and Captain George was sailing his ship from London to New York when he was blown out of his regular route and his ship was wrecked on the rocks of St. George Island. He and his men had the choice of staying on his ship and drowning, or going ashore and facing the devils, so they decided to go ashore. They found, to their surprise, a beautiful country with all kinds of tropical fruit trees and vegetables. They rescued what they could from the ship and started to build houses for themselves. Later they built a small ship of Cedar trees and returned to England. It then became known that the devils and evil spirits had left the Islands and it was now safe to go there.

English immigrants started to settle on the Islands, Later, Negroes and former slaves came and then Portuguese. When George landed, the Islands were overrun with wild pigs and it is supposed, when they were first discovered, that someone - probably the pirates - brought pigs here. The pirates spread the rumors about the devils so that they could use the Islands as their own. Later, the pirates were shot or drowned, and when George got there he found only pigs. He really discovered the Islands for the second time, and started to settle them.

These Islands are not all summer and sun as you can see from my letters. We have many cold and rainy days, but without the rain it would soon be impossible to live here. When two Bermudians meet here they will first ask to the other's health, and the next question is " Have you plenty of water?" and if you have water you guard it. Some poor Bermudians that want to build a house will mark off a square and start sawing out the coral to make the cellar that will be the cistern for the water, and then they will use the coral blocks sawed out to build the walls and roof. The cistern has to be lined with cement to be waterproof. The big Hotels here buy a cliffside, clean it off of shrubs and dirt, then line it with cement, whitewash it and use the water that falls there, collecting it in big tanks at the bottom. No glass is needed for windows in the native huts as a lot of houses only have a square hole with a shutter for a window.

The houses look nice and white, but must be whitewashed every year to stay nice. The stone gets a gray color after being exposed to sun and weather. The roofs have to be whitewashed once a year by law to prevent epidemics from dirty water, and all these white roofs are especially beautiful at night with the moon throwing light on them.

Here we are farther South than New York, in fact as far South as Northern Africa. The sun is farther overhead in the daytime and the moon is big and bright at night. The houses look like snow banks in the distance, and you almost have to touch the roof to make sure it isn't snow. The Bermudians that have been nowhere else have never seen snow, and don't understand it - most only know snow from pictures.

Here are a lot of fishermen - they fish around the Islands and then go to New York and sell the catch. The ground is red - that is iron in the dirt, and some natives dig down to the rock where the dirt is more red, then take some of it and mix it with water, then let it stand to clear and drink it to get the iron.

You find no moles or snakes here, but plenty of ants and birds. I see mostly two kinds of birds around Paynhurst; a red one, a cardinal is so puffy and plentiful; and then a blue one they call bluebird - and you can hear them all day saying "All right - All right - All right". The ants are all over and get in the houses. Wherever there is food they will try to get it before you do. In the house's kitchens everything has to be kept in tin containers, and the kitchen table has to have tin cups of water under each leg to keep the ants off it. You don't see any anthills, but they are all over, and if one ant discovers a piece of bread or any food, in a few minutes there will be 1000's of them. If there is nothing to eat, you don't notice them, and you think they have gone away, but they are there.

The banana trees grow to a height of 6-8 feet, and it takes about one year to grow a stalk with bananas. When they are ripe you cut it down and a new one comes up.

I think I told you I saw a show called "Neptune's Daughter" with Annette Kellerman that was taken here, and the scenes from the cave were at Crystal Cave. I am planning to get there and see it, also to a place called "Devils Hole" that is stocked with all kinds of colorful fish from around here.

Some places where the poor people have no horses they will use two men to pull a cultivator or plow, and it seems to work out all right.

The best to all

Hal

March 30, 1917
Bermuda

Mr. Hues has gone home and we have lost our milkman, so the cow was sold, but we are now getting close to the end here - almost another month. The "Bermudian" is now carrying a big load of Easter Lilies every trip, besides all other fresh vegetables. In May, the farmers will again plant and sow, hoping for a summer crop, but sometimes it fails on account of no rain, and it dries up. Some let the farm rest in the summertime and they go fishing to get some money.

The Bermudians have no use for the modern rush - they like things as they are, so if they have enough to eat today, why worry about tomorrow? Put your good clothes on and go to town and buy a glass of beer!

I just got a letter from you and I am sorry to hear Dad is not feeling really good and is giving up the teaching job, and you are moving to an apartment in Copenhagen. I have taken a lot of pictures here and I am glad I had the chance to get here, but now I will be glad to go to New York. Now I wish Dad can be better with the specialist in Copenhagen, and I hope the good weather now in the Spring and Summer will help.

The best to you all

Hal

Lis Clark

Friday, April 6, 1917
Bermuda

Dearest all

Today it is Easter Friday and I am sitting in my room as we have a cold wind blowing and it is cloudy and looks like it could start to rain anytime. We have two holidays for Easter, today and then Easter Sunday, and that is it. I can sit here by the window and see out over the Atlantic Ocean and see the waves showing white as far out as I can see, but that is not as far as when the weather is clear, and the ocean is in an angry mood. I am keeping inside as much as I can, as I want to stay dry because here the rain comes down hard and then suddenly it is over again.

Frank took the horse out and went to Hamilton. The time is 2:35 p.m. and I sit and think about you over there on the other side of all that water, and I always look for mail when the ship comes in, as it will Monday. The "Bermudian" has to make one more trip and then it is our turn to go North, and that is good. I am getting to feel lonesome here. I think maybe I miss Marie, at least I could visit with her. I would not want to live here all year around. The summer can get rather hot and still damp. The people here don't know the joy of seeing a tree and a whole forest come to life and start with little green spears coming out and turn into green leaves. Of course, the trees here get new leaves also, only you don't see them any more than you do on an Evergreen up North. The new leaves are there among all the old, big leaves, and the tree looks the same all year around. There are mostly cedar trees here and they look somewhat like an evergreen. The flowers here are beautiful, but it is the same always, and I will soon be back in New York State just in time to see the trees unfold their best beauty now in May.

I wish I could get some good Rye bread (Pumpernickel). The stuff we get here is terrible, and I am getting tired of eating Gingerbread.

Now the roads in Denmark have started to dry up and be passable. Here they are dry 1/2 hour after a heavy rain. The water just disappears.

I have been on a trip to the "Crystal Cave" and I will try to tell you about it now when I have the time. It was last Sunday and I went to Hamilton and rented a bicycle for Sunday afternoon for 1/2 crown, which is 2 1/2 shillings or about 65 cent. I had my camera with me and two sandwiches in my pocket, also a small square of ginger cake, so I had something to keep me going for the afternoon of hard pumping up and down the hills. The roads here are narrow, but excellent as everything has to be transported on the roads by horse and wagon or by boat and the government has spent a lot of money on improving the roads. Some hills are cut down; they do that with a saw and the rocks are used to build a nice railing along the roads and a cement ditch takes care of the water. When it rains, the roads get washed clean and the water runs down the ditches and out through a hole in the wall or railing and disappears in the fields and in a 1/2 hour after a rain the roads are clean and dry.

I started from Hamilton 12 noon and struggled over some hills that are not yet cut down. It was a nice warm day and I took the long way around the South shore to see as much as possible. It was a beautiful road that went out along the shore, sometimes hanging halfway up the side of the cliffs and at other times curved inland with Palmettos along the ditch and view over little 5-8 acres farms where the land was divided into squares with different kinds of vegetables growing in each square. The road went on through small villages with gardens full of flowers out to the road and picket fences - also usually a church in the center of the town. The cemetery is around the Church and all the graves have a flat stone cover over a hole cut in the ground, in which the casket is placed. The stone cover is cemented in place, and then white washed and has an inscription on it. It is about 1 to 11/2 feet above the ground.

I am getting hot pumping that bicycle as I still go up and down the hills and have to be careful to keep to the left. There is not much traffic and when I rest along the road a wagon full of Negroes goes by followed by more wagons and Negroes - a whole string of them. They are on a Sunday outing and some are singing, others talking and laughing. They are grinning and waving to me and I got the impression they felt sorry for me working the cycle while they were riding in style. I waved back to them and I was glad I was there to see them enjoy themselves.

I continued, and soon the road went through a place with hedges on both sides, hedges of flowering Oleanders, and I could see the Cardinals (People call them "redbird") flying in and out of the bushes, they were so beautiful with red feathers and a crown on their heads, and they keep calling "all right - all right - all right". The "Crystal Cave" was not too far away, but they don't open till 4 p.m. on account of wartime restrictions on use of electricity, so I stopped and got a drink of water at a house, and ate my sandwich, then I continued to the cave entrance. I bought my ticket and joined about six other people for the first guided tour today in the world's wonder cave.

We were at the bottom of a hill and a tunnel went straight in the hill, but so far it was dark (no electricity yet) so we waited. Suddenly a little bulb over the entrance came to life. The guide turned a switch and the tunnel lit up with small bulbs some distance apart. We could see the tunnel was out through the rock and we walked in following the guide. The path went in and slightly downhill; after about 100 feet we could feel the air getting damp and cool. We went down a few steps and then continued down for some distance and we came to the end of the lights and it was dark ahead. The guide stopped and we all bunched up behind him. Then he said "Ladies and Gentlemen - here you see one of the earth's wonders", but it was dark and we could see nothing. The guide was trying to do something and he must have done the right thing for the whole place lit up, and we could see we were standing on a path with a rock wall on each side and a roof up high over our heads. The rock wall on one side was sort of leaning over and it was all wet and the water was dripping from it. Stone icicles protruded from the roof and the water over thousands of years had made the stone tops in different colors. The lights were placed so they showed the colors to the best advantage.

The guide showed us different formations and one looked like a bird nest with birds in it and a bird standing on the edge. He said he went down in the cave every day and often discovered something new. We walked some more and there, far away, we could see a giant butterfly sitting on the rock wall and it seemed to move. It had two pair of wings as butterflies have. Behind the wings were lights and the wings were so thin that the light was showing through. The light turned red and we were sure the wings moved.

We walked on and came to a big room, went down a few steps and came to a pond where the water was 40 feet deep. A bridge went out on the water and we could stand there and see down. The water was so clear, like air, so we could see the bottom with stones and rocks just like it was within our reach. This water is fresh and has no connection with the ocean. He claimed it was the only natural water on the Islands. Now the guide turned some switches and all the lights came on and we could see the cave was about 100 feet long and 40 feet high and the formations were hanging down from the roof like curtains. We could see all the points hanging down with a drop of water on the ends. Some were thin and some a couple of feet in diameter, and we could hear the drip, drip, drip. The formations are growing down from the roof and also up from the floor and some meet halfway up. It is a beautiful cave and it was discovered only about ten years ago, and it was here Annette Kellerman, in the film "Neptune's Daughter"[9] swam and made this

---

9   On researching this movie, I found only a reference to Jamaica but some scenes may have been filmed in Bermuda without acknowledgement

place known all over the world. In the film she was swimming across the pond looking for the witch that lived in the cave.

I enjoyed the trip and got back home tired and late, and tomorrow I have to get up 1 hour earlier as we have to set our clocks to the fast summer time. I will have to mail this tomorrow to get it on the ship this week.

Love to all

Hal

Monday April 9, 1917

Today I got my mail. "The Bermudian" came in Saturday and I didn't expect the mail so quick, but it was not censored, so it went right through. I received a letter from my friend Jens Christensen - it has been since New Years getting here but no letter from you. I am thinking that the Germans could stop the ships from going to Denmark, but I hope that is not the case. I have to continue tomorrow.

Tuesday April 10, 1917

Today I had an important surprise. For me, it meant time off; for the United States it must be important or they would not do it for me; it also meant contact with Denmark, and this letter is going to reach you by special delivery by Danish Destroyer Warship. Here is how the events of the day went.

Frith came home from Hamilton and told me a warship was in the harbor and it had a strange flag on the mast. Someone told him it was a Danish ship, so he rushed home to ask me to take a look at it, as the flag was red with a white cross. So I said "It must be Danish" and we both went up in the tower on the big house where we could see all over the harbor and city of Hamilton. We saw a ship, it looked like a destroyer with a Danish flag straight out in the wind and there was no doubt about it, it was the Danish flag, old "Dannebrog" as the flag is called by Danes. I suddenly got an overpowering urge to get aboard and stay there to go home, but I knew I couldn't. I rushed down from the tower and got a hold of Mr. Payn - told him about the ship and that I had to go to Hamilton and meet it or contact somebody from the ship. It was the "Valkyrien" from the West Indies "Virgin Islands" on the way home to Denmark. I am going to try to get this letter home with it so you will get it in a few days instead of months, so I will go to Hamilton and bring this letter with me. I am fine but I am terribly homesick for home.

Hal

April 19, 1917
Bermuda

I have had a big surprise as I told you in my letter, and now, more than a week late I am again settled down so I can think.

I got mail today - postcard from Marie and a card from Solveig - both from the week of March 10. It is getting close to the time for us to start packing and leaving all this behind, as we will be on the "Bermudian's" next trip out, so I am asking Frith to mail any mail to me back to Chatham.

But I will tell you about the visit here of the "Valkyrien" Danish destroyer warship now leaving as the Virgin Islands now belong to the United States. I went to Hamilton harbor and met two men from the ship and was I excited - it was a real thrill to talk Danish again. The two men were machinist N.P. Soerensen, Delfingade 22, Copenhagen and A.G. Tjoernquist, Svensensgade 60, Copenhagen. They invited me aboard and they told me to come again the next day for lunch 12 o'clock noon for a real Danish lunch, with pumpernickel, rullepolse (this is a Danish sandwich meat) and Danish cheese. I got a tour of the ship and then went home, promising to get there for lunch.

N.P. Soerensen, Hal and A.G. Tjoernquist aboard the "Valkyrien"

The "Valkyrien" had been to the Virgin Islands on account of the trouble with the Negroes there, and now that the Islands had been sold, they were going home and they were all glad to get back. Well, I met them for the lunch – I had told Mr. Payn and he said "Sure, go when you can", so I really enjoyed it. I was introduced to a lot of officers and the Captain, and had lunch in the officers' mess with them. Tablecloths on the table, sailors waiting on us, schnapps and Danish beer, and when I left they gave me a 12 pound loaf of Pumpernickel. With that under my arm, I said good-bye to my friends, gave them your address. I was sorry to see them go. Everyone was nice and we had a good time.

They had been in the Virgin Islands for one and a half years trip and were also glad to be going back home. They were here to load coal for the trip across the Atlantic and were here two days. That was a good experience and I was wishing they could stay longer.

By now you should have the letter they brought with them and they also said they would visit you so you could talk with them. I took some pictures and I am sending some there. This will be the last letter from here as we are leaving on the next ship out, where this letter also will be aboard.

Everyone talks about the danger of going on the ship now as submarines have been seen over here. Last Wednesday, they tried to torpedo an American ship outside New York but missed. As our ship is English it is fair game, but we have to get back and are told we will be escorted by American Destroyers.

I will send my next letter from New York. Hope you are all well.

Hal

CHAPTER SEVEN

We Say Goodby To Bermuda

Monday April 23, 1917
On board SS Bermudian

Now we are on the way to New York after a hectic couple of days. We left Hamilton this morning after spending some time getting everything ready. Frank had some big wooden crate that we packed with the gear and blankets for the horses and then our own trunks were ready. Dick, Firth's brother, came before six o'clock a.m. to get us and the horses, as most of the trunks from the house and ours were brought to the ship the day before.

Frank and I got in the back of Dick's wagon and led our three horses that ran behind over to the ship. We got unloaded and the horses were put aboard. Then Frank couldn't find our tickets that Mrs. Payn had given him the day before, and he suddenly remembered they were in his uniform pocket and were packed with the blankets and other stuff for the horses, and it was already brought to the boat yesterday. On deck the cranes were now loading trunks and lowering them in the hold, so we went there and looked down the hatch to see if we could locate the box, but we couldn't and as we were standing there looking down, Frank with his mouth open, suddenly lost his upper dentures. They slipped out of his mouth, went down the hold among all the trunks. They would not let us go down there to look for them, but the men tried to find them, and we stopped the work for a while. But the teeth were gone, and we had no tickets.

The ship was scheduled to leave in 20 minutes, so we were told to get to the Steamship Office and get duplicate tickets. We ran all the way there, got a paper that permitted us to travel and ran all the way back. We just got aboard when they removed the gangplank, so they must have been waiting for us. We were on our way without tickets and Frank without teeth.

It was a little windy this first day, but I am not seasick. If it gets worse, I may have to go to bed, but now it is 5 p.m. and I am soon going up to dinner, so I am sure eating all I can while I feel good. Tomorrow it may be different, when we get in the Gulfstream. I will write more, later.

Hal

April 25, 1917
New York

We arrived here today after a fair trip. We had the wind at our back going home and the old "Bermudian" was making good time and moving, slowly tipping from side to side as she went through the waves and I didn't miss a meal all the way to New York. We didn't see any submarines and no destroyers either. Frank didn't enjoy the trip, he couldn't eat all the steak he had planned to "no teeth".

I am staying a couple of days here in New York. First, to help Frank to get the horses moved through New York and put on the Riverboat, and then to go to the factory to get the car and drive it to Chatham. The trees are just now beginning to show big buds over here, and the bushes have small leaves, and I am freezing as my overcoat is packed in the box with Frank's stuff and our tickets. I lost my camera on the dock when I put it down for a minute to help Mrs. Payn to open her trunks. When I turned back to pick it up it was not there any more.

We got everything through the Customs and I went out and bought another camera. Tomorrow we will get the horses and Mr. and Mrs. Payn are going to Chatham by train. I have to get the car and drive it to Chatham and Frank has to go with the horses and buy himself new teeth when he gets to Chatham.

The best to you all

Hal

After thought- I must tell you many people including Mrs. Payn never went to bed on the trip from Bermuda, but slept in a chair and all the lifeboats were swung out and ready to be lowered at a moment's notice.

Hal

Sunday April 29, 1917
Chatham New York

Dear Mom and Dad

I am now back in Chatham where I arrived from New York about 2:30 a.m. this morning. This is Sunday evening and I have a little time to write before going to bed; it always seems I get caught driving that road from New York at night, so now I can find it at night as well as in the daytime. I spent a few days in New York and when everything was done it was Saturday afternoon and 4 p.m. before I left New York and I made good time to Poughkeepsie - 75 miles - where I stopped at 7 p.m. to eat and for a cup of coffee for 30-40 minutes.

Then, it was way North again, and the weather was getting cold and damp, and I saw snow in the ditches. Only 1/2 hour out of Poughkeepsie the car broke down and there I was in the dark, and something was wrong with the gearshift. I tried to fix it, but I couldn't without tools and light, so I got it so I could use high gear, and I managed to go the rest of the way, and somehow got up all the hills by speeding and I got to Chatham 2 a.m., so now I have to have a mechanic from the factory in New York up here to fix it. I am tired from the long ride last night, and I will take a little nap now. I am glad to be back to Mrs. Stupplebeen's cooking. I can't stand my own cooking any more.

The best of wishes to you all

Hal

Sunday May 5, 1917

Dear All,

Today it is Sunday again and I see in the paper it looks bad for all the small countries around Germany as the blockade also keeps ships from reaching them, and it also told a story about a revolution in Sweden, and two battleships were ready to take the Royal Swedish Family to England if it is getting worse, but I don't believe it as the Scandinavians are level headed people and they love their King and Queen; if that is possible in Sweden it could also happen in Denmark and I think it is the Socialist that are making trouble.

Denmark is sending food to Germany and they are also doing it in Norway so they can get their ships torpedoed. Norway has lost 63 ships from English submarines, and will have no ships left when the summer is past, but as long as they can they will supply Germany with food to keep Germany from attacking them. I understand the Danish ships have stopped sailing to USA, so can the mail go some other way? I am expecting some letters from you that have been to Bermuda as Frith will return them to me here. If I get a letter tomorrow, I will continue this letter.

Hal

Tuesday May 7, 1917

As I expected, I got mail today, not alone what I expected, but a bonus of four letters and one postcard that had been to Bermuda. They were all mailed in the month of March and took two months to get here. So, my sister Adda is now planning to get married in the fall. I sure would like to get home for that party as I have missed a few by now, but even if I would like to go very much, it is not possible now under these conditions.

Mr. Payn has bought one more automobile in New York on the way home from Bermuda. It is the same kind as the one we have, an Owen-Magnetic, but this is a used one that belonged to Mr. Vanderbilt, so someday soon I will have to go to New York and get it.

It is now ten days since I came back to Chatham and it has rained most of the time. We have not been able to drive the car on the roads around here - they are terrible, cut up with sinkholes and you risk getting stuck. Mr. and Mrs. Payn went to Albany today on the train. I hope they will use the other car more, as that is not so heavy and from now on the roads will be better and summer is just around the corner.

That is all and that was not much

Hal

May 12, 1917
Chatham

I have not been to New York to get the other automobile, but it will be soon. We have been out with the other car on a couple of short trips - to Albany one day and Kinderhook another day. The weather is getting better and the roads are drying up. I mailed a souvenir book of postcards the other day, but it came back, as it was not allowed in the mail at this time.

I have also been to the dentist in Chatham. He filled five teeth and charged five dollars. A lot of people here have their teeth filled with gold and some get gold crowns put on their teeth, so it shines when they smile - it is even used on dentures. Americans like it, but I think it looks artificial.

Love to all

Hal

May 20, 7:30 p.m., 1917
Chatham

I just finished my supper and now have time to write before bedtime, and it is still light enough to do it before the sun goes down. It is now three weeks since we came back from Bermuda and today is the first real nice summer day. The poor weather this Spring has kept us from using the car very much, so I have not had much work and I have helped Mr. Stupplebeen in the garden, planting trees and cutting grass, but now it looks like better weather is coming, so today Mr. and Mrs. Payn wanted a little ride and we went to Kinderhook to Mrs. Payn's mother's place. Mr. Ogden and his wife came there also, and I got a chance to talk to them. He had a new car he bought for his wife. The trees are now out full and fresh green. The cherry trees are in blossom and everywhere people are busy in their gardens. The gardens here are different from the gardens in Denmark. Here a garden is just a lawn in front of the house and a walk from the street straight up to the front porch - very seldom is there any hedge around it where in Denmark you see no front porch and the garden is surrounded by a hedge and laid out in walks with bushes and flowerbeds, sometimes a circular lawn around a flagpole in the center, but just a small lawn, if any.

This year a lot of people dig up the backyard and try to raise vegetables as this country is now getting in the War and shortages are beginning to show here and there in the food line. Hope you are all feeling better now that spring is here. I live in the same room at Stupplebeen's that I had last year and enjoy the cooking. Always plenty to eat and they are nice people. I am getting to know the neighbors. Dr. Walker, a dentist, lives across the street - he took care of my teeth.

Love to all

Hal

June 10, 1917
Chatham, New York

Dear all

Now the weather is getting better - I have been kept busy and I work every day. If I want to go somewhere I must tell Mrs. Payn to get time off, except in the evening. I received a couple of letters from you and things look bad over there as well as here. I had to go and report to an office set up in Chatham as we now are going to send troops to Europe and everyone between the ages of 21-30 must report and have their name down. I went there and came back with a small card with my name on and a number. They tell me they are not going to use me as I look like a German and it is only American citizens they can use as soldiers.

The 13th of June I have been here one year, and I can take out my first papers to apply for citizenship. I have been to New York to get another car Mr. Payn bought, but it is not satisfactory. The first car is good and it will go about 65-70 miles per hour and it starts good as I very seldom have to turn the crank more than a couple of turns to get it going. The new car is an open sports model, but it is a used one that belonged to Mr. Vanderbilt and Mr. Vanderbilt has run the life out of it.

Well, I went down to New York and got it and Mr. Payn's son met me there to ride back to Chatham with me and he didn't like the car. He said his father had no business to buy a used car. We drove to Chatham in four hours and that was going as fast as the road would allow. The road is winding with one curve after another all the way and it seems about 100 little villages to go through and young Payn said give it all it will take and let us see if it is any good, but even on level road it would only go 65 mph. Mr. Payn was sitting in the back seat with a hand clamped on each side to keep in the seat as the road was full of holes and bumps. When I looked back to see if he was still there after some severe bumps, he would say "Never mind me, I am hanging on - just let her go", so I did that and we made it in four hours. He is a stout, big man and he was flying off the seat more than sitting in it.

I am enclosing some pictures from Chatham and I enclose a note to Solveig. I counted the pictures she has taken and sent me during the winter, there were 26 so she has been doing good with her camera.

I have no use for formal clothes. Smoking and jacket suits, they are not used in Chatham so I am packing them away till I get home again. We have a lot of rain now, but that will stop soon and we will have hot summer again. I wish I could have been with you to the birthday party on "La Reine" for Soren's birthday. I could go for that "Smorgasbord" - the food here is tiresome, not much variety and that is not Mrs. Stupplebeen's cooking, she is doing the best she can, but I can see it in the grocery store. They never have more than the same local cheese, and it is always the same white bread and bologna. You never see fish around here and the only dessert is pie. I miss you all.

Solveig is now out of high school with excellent marks she writes, so congratulations.

Love to all Hal

June 24, 1917
Chatham

It is now two weeks since I sent my last letter. I have been too busy to write so you will know no letter from last week is missing. I had a letter from sister Adda, she told me old Jens Jensen died. It seems a lot of old people have died since I left one year ago, and I can't keep track of all these people, but I will miss them when I get back.

The new car has been sitting in the barn for a week now without being used, so Mr. Payn sent me to New York with it to return it, he didn't want it and that was good - I didn't like it either and Mr. Payn has plenty of money so he can buy a new car, he doesn't need to use an old warn out car that may give us trouble. So, that car is gone and I came back this time by train. We have been to Albany twice this week to visit the Governor Whitman. Albany is the capitol city, and the Capitol Building and the Governor's Mansion is there. But I don't understand the politics here, it seems Mr. Payn is the leader and tells the governor what to do. Mr. Stupplebeen tells me very few people understand or know Mr. Payn has a power over all the big politicians from the top and down.

He was a high ranking republican and he is said to be the one that decides who is to be Governor and President. Teddy Roosevelt is a friend of his and also President Wilson, that has been President since 1913. Mr. Payn has his men working all over the country in all kinds of political jobs and he gets reports from them. Often men come here to talk with him and I hear them talking in the car and they will ask him for a big job in the State or Federal Government and they get it if Mr. Payn promises them the job. There is a General Heley, one of

Mr. Payn's friends. He was a Captain, but Mr. Payn had him elevated to General because he asked him for it, over the head of other men standing in line for that job.

The roads in New York State are a mess and now with a car Mr. Payn finds out about it, so I heard him say "The roads are getting worse every year, especially from Chatham to New York. I am going to Albany Monday, and see the Governor about it, and it will take me two hours to straighten that out, and if the roads don't get better soon some heads are going to roll".

Mr. Payn was on a trip out West somewhere and came back to Albany to change trains to get to Chatham on the Boston and Albany Railroad. A train was ready to leave Albany for Boston, but it was an express that doesn't stop in Chatham, and the next local train was not due to leave for two hours, so Mr. Payn demanded a seat on the express and ordered the stationmaster to have the train stop in Chatham to let him off. The station master refused so Mr. Payn telegraphed the President of the railroad and got on the train. By the time the train got to Chatham the station master they had his orders and he stopped the train so Mr. Payn could get off, so it looks like he gets what he wants. I will write again soon. I am still worrying a little about the War and how I stand on being drafted. I hope I don't hear any more about it.

Love to all

Hal

July 6, 1917
Chatham, New York

The fourth of July is a big day here, with fireworks and speeches and parades. In Chatham there were some booths set up and they were selling balloons, ice cream, candy, cigars and roasted frankfurters - you know them, they come in a string of them, small but good eating - everything sold, the money goes to the Red Cross to help the boys now starting to go overseas to war. Every letter I get now has been opened and even the lining inside the envelopes have been taken out, so you better get envelopes without lining.

One of the boarders here at Stupplebeen's is Mr. Snow. He works at The Borden Co. He has been telling me about milk and I am always interested in everything that goes on around me. The Borden Co. owns farms and bottling plants all over the country. On their farms they have prized milk cows and they take special care and precautions to lower the bacteria count in the milk from their farms so they can label it Grade A milk and sell it raw for more money than they get for farmer's milk sold as Grade B. Farmers milk is pasteurized, but their own milk is not as it is not needed. They have milk wagons picking up the milk around the countryside every day. Some is put in tin cans and some is bottled and sent to the big cities. From here it goes to New York City. The State has inspectors visiting the farms and the Bottling plant to check on the milk. Borden farms produce the best possible milk. The cows are washed and currycombed every morning before milking and the men have to wash their hands before milking each cow. At night before milking the cows have to be washed again. The cow's head and horns get washed every day also.

The milk gets cooled with ice that is kept in big Icehouses that get harvested in the wintertime. The men that do the milking get paid well. Mr. Snow gets 35$ a month and they pay for his board and room, but he has to work 11 hours every day including Sunday. For overtime he gets 25 cents an hour and he often has to work extra hours.

I had a talk with Mr. Payn the other day. I work every day also including Sunday and I am on call also evenings so I asked him to give me more money, and we agreed on a $10.00 raise from $35 to $45 dollars a month, and then he has been paying $6 dollars for my board and room per week, so he is going to give me $25 dollars more per month, and that takes care of that.

Mr. Payn is now building a new garage, big enough for three cars and a room upstairs I can use if I want to, but it will take all summer to finish it and I will, I think, stick to Mrs. Stupplebeen's cooking. It looks like I am all set for the summer now, but I don't want to go to Bermuda again this winter to work for less money, so we will see what happens - I am sure something will.

I can't understand the girls in Bermuda were always complaining about Payn's being tight and starving them; I have no trouble with them and I also think they are anxious to keep me here. When Frank wanted something for the horses he had trouble getting it, but I need tools, oil or other things and I just go and buy it and give Mrs. Payn the bill and she pays me and never mentions the expenses or the need for it.

That is all for this week.

Love to all

Hal

July 22, 1917
Chatham, New York

Dear all

I have received a lot of mail that I thought was missing. Thanks for everything. I see Dad has been to the doctor again, I hope he is feeling good now again, and I understand he has a relief teacher doing his work. Now the vacation is coming up, Aug. 1 to Sept. 1, so Dad will not have to work till that is over and he can get a good rest in August.

Here the children go to school from 9 to 12 and 1 to 4, but not on Saturday or Sunday and they have a long summer vacation - about 2 1/2 months - and long vacations for Christmas and Easter, so they don't get much schooling, but then they can continue going till they are `18 years old, so that makes up for it. Some children quit school when they are 16 years old, but that is not so good.

We now have nice, warm weather, but rain and thundershowers about every day that cools it off. Today it was 90 degree. in the shade and that is warm, the warmest so far for this year.

The War is still going strong and all the young men are going to training for six weeks and then shipped to England or France. Mrs. Payn had a Garden Party to raise some money for The Red Cross. 50 children were here and put on a little show and in the evening she showed some slides about the Red Cross activity and served strawberries and Ice Cream. She raised $150 for the Red Cross.

I am kept on my toes now driving, but not so long trips. We go somewhere every day, if not to Albany, Kinderhook, Great Barrington or Hudson, then we take just a ride on the country roads around here as it is very beautiful country with great views at every turn of the road. We have been to Queechee Lake and Lebanon Mountains. When we get back I am tired and have to start cleaning the car so it is shining for the next day.

I had a card from Marie in Jutland Denmark, she has been on a vacation to Skagen.

Love to you all - have a good vacation.

Hal

August 1, 1917
Chatham, New York

Dear all

Received no mail since I last wrote and we now have such hot weather that we are ready to give it up and just go swimming. We have had no rain since my last letter and continued heat, and it seems to come out of the ground. It was 94 degrees this morning at 9 a.m. and now at 12 noon it is 98 degrees in the shade. I sleep on top of the bed nights, but not too good in that heat, and I am dripping with sweat as I sit here writing.

Mr. and Mrs. Stupplebeen and all the children from the Sunday school in the Lutheran Church had a picnic in the woods, a lot of people from the Church were there - also the Waltermire family that lives next door here on the street - Hudson Ave. We brought a big basket with food and we went swimming in the creek and waterhole. I know the Waltermire's as they are always inviting me to come in and visit and play cards with them.

The Waltermire Family

Later, same day

No mail yet, but I expect to hear you are going somewhere for the vacation month of August. It is now 7 p.m. and it feels a little cooler; this noon I had to give up writing in the heat. The only time I feel comfortable is when I drive and get the wind in my face from the speed of the car. Not much happening so I send my love to you all.

Hal

August 8, 1917
Chatham

I received your letter and a postcard from Adda. The heat is not so bad now. We had a big thunderstorm and a lot of rain, that helped to cool things off. I have been teaching the Waltermire's next door to drive. he bought a car, but none of them know anything about driving it, Here you don't need a license to drive a car unless you are a chauffeur, so I have been taking them out on little trips evenings and now they can drive it. There is Mr. and Mrs. Waltermire and Mrs. Waltermire's sister that stays with them, Miss Margaret Kruse. Now they can go out by themselves. There is not much traffic on the roads so they get along all right. Some people are trying to drive and don't know how so they are weaving from side to side and you also see 12-14 year old children drive, but they all learn it without any trouble. It is not a good thing so I think they will soon have Driver Licenses for everyone.

Love to all

Hal

August 26, 1917
Chatham, New York

Dear all

I received some letters from you that have been two months on the way; also some pictures from Solveig. Some are not very good - too dark, you need more sun and that is sometimes hard to get in Denmark. Solveig is now finished with her school and Adda may get married soon. I seem to miss a lot by being here, but now there is no way to get home.

I was over to Kinderhook last Saturday night and watched the concert on the Bandstand in the village square and there was quite a crowd. I saw two young men I seemed to know so I walked over to them and I heard them talking Danish. I spoke to them and found out they were working for Mr. Ogden and they had been in this country since last year and I knew them because they came here on the same ship I came here with, so we had a long talk about the trip and they had traveled together and worked here and there on farms.

On Monday Sept. 3, we are going to have the yearly market and fair in Chatham. It usually lasts five days and I am looking forward to it as they have horse races and a Midway with all kinds of games and the highlight will be a speech by former President Theodore Roosevelt. Mr. Payn has invited him to come here and stay for dinner. He was President of the United States from 1901 - 1909 due mostly to Mr. Payn's efforts and they tell me he is quite a character, so I look forward to meeting him and get the honor of driving for him.

Mrs. Payn's mother died suddenly in Kinderhook Friday night, and one of the girls working for Mrs. Payn came to get me at Stupplebeen's in the middle of the night so I could drive Payn's to Kinderhook at 3 a.m.. Mrs. Payn was crying and Mr. Payn was grumbling about getting up in the middle of the night.

Mrs. Payn has been talking about going on a trip to the White Mountains. I think they are in New Hampshire, but that is canceled now and I wouldn't get that trip. You know, trips like that are just like a vacation for me as I enjoy it as much as they do and everything is free for me. As the Americans say "It's on the house".

My birthday, August 19, came and went and I entirely forgot it. That is the first time that happened. I remembered about it two days later; well I could not celebrate anyway. After the Fair, in about two weeks I will write again so till then so long.

Later

I am still thinking about my forgotten birthday. I remember as a child I could hardly wait for it, it was the highlight of summer to me and the fact it always came during our vacation made it better and you,

Mom and Dad, always made it a special day for me. I never thought it would ever be different, but as we get older things change. For one day I would like to go back to that time. I miss you all.

Love

Hal

Next I will write about the Fair and Teddy Roosevelt.

CHAPTER EIGHT

Meeting "Teddy"

Sept. 7, 1917
Chatham, New York

Thanks for all the letters and cards wishing me a Happy Birthday. I got cards from Dad, Adda, Solveig, Grandmother and a big package of newspapers. One letter was missing, the one from Mom, but then I will get that next week.

Our big Fair is now over and I had time to go there and enjoy myself. The highlight was "Teddy" coming here and it seems the whole village was out to receive him and hear his speech. "Teddy" was President from 1901 till 1909 and before that governor of New York State from 1899 to 1901.

Lis Clark

I had the car shined up and polished, inside and out, and Mr. Payn went with me to the train station to pick him up. The weather was fine and a parade was organized with 25-30 automobiles all dressed up with flags and Mr. Payn's car was at the front. The train pulled in and Mr. Payn got out of the car and waited for "Teddy" to come out and down the steps. It must have been a special train, because "Teddy" and some State Troopers came out, no other passengers. He shook hands with Mr. Payn and then we started for Mr. Payn's estate, where they got out and went in the house.

The other cars in the Parade stopped behind and some men from them also went in the house. It must have been State Officials and local politicians. After about 1/2 hour they all came out, got in the cars - Mr. Payn and Mr. Roosevelt in the back seat and Mrs. Payn in the front seat with me. Now we drove slowly followed by all the cars to the Fairground that was packed with people.

We took one turn around the Racetrack and then stopped at the Grandstand where all the celebrities got out. A platform with a speaker's stand was erected in front of the grandstand and Teddy, Mr. Payn and a lot of other men got on the stand to start the celebration and speeches. I was sorry I missed the main event as I had to drive the car away and over on the other side of the track followed by all the other cars.

After the speeches, I was called back and again picked up the ex President, and Mr. and Mrs. Payn, to go back to the Payn's house for the dinner. Now we had a car with an orchestra in front playing, then I came with my cargo and then the tail of 25 cars. At the house "Teddy" got out and stood at the stairs. He shook hands with several hundred people that had followed us. Then they went in the house to eat, before it was time to return to the station to board the train. The whole string of cars followed us to the train station and there was more handshaking.

Just before getting on the train "Teddy" said "Now there is one more man I wish to meet and shake hands with, and that is the man behind the steering wheel". So Mr. Payn presented me to "Teddy", told him my name and that I was from Denmark and we shook hands and I said I was glad to meet him. That was nice, but I guess that took the place of a tip. Ha Ha! "Teddy" got on the train, it was getting late and I was glad to go home and get my dinner.

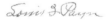

Hon. Louis F. Payn *Ex President Theodore Roosevelt*

The trip to White Mountains is not being mentioned anymore so that is still off. I had a letter from Nielsen, the officer from "Valkyrien" that I went for a walk with in Bermuda. He is going to try and visit you soon. Today we were on a trip to Troy and then to Albany and back to Chatham - we did it all this forenoon, about 80 miles so this afternoon I washed the car and just before 5 p.m. I went to the train station to pick up some guests.

The weather has been turning colder now and it is close to frost at night, but warm sunshine days, not bad. Tomorrow, it is Mom's birthday, I will think of you, in fact I do that every day. Good night now it is time for bed.

Love, Hal

Sept. 19, 1917

Dear all

No letters since last I wrote and Mom's birthday letter to me didn't get here yet, it is just one month overdue now so I am looking for it every day when I get home for lunch after the mailman has been here. We have now cold weather and night frost. I see in the papers I got that Sweden and Denmark have some real trouble staying out of the War. It is getting bad here too, with all the young men going off to fight and have to leave their jobs in factories and offices. Then, immigrants, some who have been here 20-30 years and never applied for citizenship now find it is possible they may pass a law that will make it possible for the government to take anybody that has been in this country for more than one year or else tell them to get out and go home. I don't blame them for that, because actually these men, including me, are benefiting by having jobs to select from, plenty of jobs all over with just few people to fill them, and I see where Scandinavian countries have trouble with too many people out of work.

Now I am keeping my fingers crossed and hope that this War will end soon. It is getting dark now as soon as dinner is over. I have missed the long summer evenings with daylight till 10-11 p.m., but now that time is also over and gone in Denmark.

Sister Adda and Soren have not yet set the date for their wedding. He promised to send me a letter last summer, but my eyes are getting very strained and tired from looking for that letter. I hope I will be able to read it when it comes. Oh well, I hope he is keeping busy.

The best to you all

Hal

Sept. 28, 1917
Chatham

Dear all

I got three postcards from Mom today sent July 27, Aug. 2 and Aug. 11 - and I see where you have read in the papers that United States is going to take foreigners living here as soldiers now soon or send them home. That is what I read in the papers here and told you about in my last letter. The law has to be passed first and then the people will get three months to sell their business or quit their jobs and leave; I don't know how they will get along here without all these thousands or millions of people that are now mostly doing the work here. I hope they will end the War before that and it doesn't look good for the Germans now.

We had a bad fire here in Chatham yesterday. The buildings on the fairground burned and all the stables are now just ashes. Mr. Payn keeps a lot of his racehorses there, sixteen were there when the fire broke out at 7 p.m., when the men were out to dinner. The buildings were all wood, well dried and the fire spread fast in a few minutes. I was there about ten minutes after it started and the fire whistle on the shirt factory nearby was blowing, but no fire truck yet. Three to four men were there trying to get some of the horses out, but they could only get three or four out, then the whole thing was a mass of flames, and 20 minutes after it started the fire truck arrived; it is a volunteer outfit and it takes time for the men to get to the firehouse - when they got there to the fire it was one hot blaze and they could not get within a hundred feet of it.

In about fifty minutes the whole thing was burned down and of the horses, there you could see what was left - it was a terrible sight. The fire was so hot it burned the skin and muscles of the horses and their feet and legs were burned off up to the knees. The skeletons and the guts were there and had to be removed. Among the four horses that were saved was a $10,000.00 racehorse and it is claimed the fire was started by someone on purpose.

Mrs. Payn told me they are not going to Bermuda this year and not again until this War ends, so they are planning on going someplace here in the United Stated where it is warm, Florida, Texas or somewhere South, and they are planning to take the car and me with them. I have heard the roads are impassable in the South for automobiles in the wintertime, but if they want to go, I will go as I would like to try the roads they say are impassable.

I forgot to tell you Mr. Payn bought another car to replace the one he sent back. This is a new sporty open car, maroon color, and I was down to New York to get it last month. It is now in the new garage that was built during the summer. It is a three car garage with heat and there is a couple of rooms upstairs, in the back is a wing of the building where Frank has charge of the four horses and all the wagons. It is nice and the old barn we have used is being torn down.

Mr. Payn is going to be 82 years old and I think Mrs. Payn is 52. We had a short summer this year. May was cold and the leaves didn't show on the trees till the 15th and June was cold and rainy. July was better and it got real hot and uncomfortable for about two weeks, then it got colder and we already had an early frost the first week of September.

Now, the end of September the leaves are already falling off the trees, so most of them are bare. More next time.

Love

Hal

$50 In My Pocket

**October 10, 1917
Chatham, New York**

Dear all

Your letter and pictures from the birthday party on my birthday. I see you are drinking to my health if not in champagne then in tea, and it was a nice picture and I can see Soren is saying "Skol". Hope you, Mom will see the doctor about your heart, but it may not be that. So you have a shortage of petroleum, so you have to save on light in your lamps at night, and no sign of the electric line coming over from Sweden, where there is plenty of electricity. When it comes is it just for Copenhagen or is there to be sent a line out to where you live ? It would be real nice if you could have electric light and even telephone but that Was is stopping all progress. Nothing about Adda and Soren getting married. Is he drafted? Did you have much fruit on your trees, and how about vegetables?

Mrs. Payn heard from someone in North Carolina that wanted them to come there for the winter, but then they found out it can get quite cold there sometimes with snow, so she didn't think that would be a good place for them to go unless they went there just for a few days and then continued further South, so I suppose it is going to be Florida - I hope.

Mrs. Black, wife of an ex-governor of New York State lives in Troy, New York and we have been to her place several times during the summer as she and her husband Governor Black were great friends of the Payn's. The ex-governor is now dead and Mrs. Black came here to visit, she is the lady we were going to see in the White Mountains in New Hampshire, but didn't go when Mrs. Payn's mother died in Kinderhook. Well, I wanted to tell you about her car.

Our car is an Owen-Magnetic, a new kind of car that has never been heard about in Europe and few people in this country know about, but Mrs. Black's car is known in this country, but not in Europe and I had never heard about it and it surprised me. It is a steamer, a car that goes by steam like a locomotive. It uses kerosene to heat the water to make steam and it is used mostly in Mountains as it is very powerful on steep roads. There are three or four factories making steamers - this is a Stanley Steamer and the used steam is cooled in the radiator and pumped back in the boiler as water so it can be used over again. It was used here in this country before the gasoline motors were known much.

As it runs on kerosene it is practical where it is hard to get gasoline and that is sometimes hard to find. Around here, you buy it in garages in the main cities, other places that have begun to install tanks are harness shops and blacksmith shops. In our new garage here on Mr. Payn's Estate we are getting our own pump so I can fill the car every morning and a truck comes and fill the underground tank. In some small villages you can buy gasoline in grocery stores that have a barrel of it in the yard, and they will fill your tank with a pail and a funnel. That is not a good way to do it and the fire hazard is great. Hope I can tell you more about our travel plans for the winter next time I write.

Love to all

Hal

October 29, 1917
Chatham, New York

Dear all

Now all your birthdays are over and I hope you have all received your Happy Birthday cards that I sent to you, Solveig in August, Dad and Mom in September and Adda in October. Well, by the time you get this it will almost be Christmas. I hope you have enough fuel to keep warm but I see all gasoline is strictly rationed and not sold for private cars unless by special permit. We have plenty of gasoline, but a shortage of sugar, but it is expected to improve after the sugar canes and sugar beets have been processed by the sugar mills. Dad wrote during the summer about a plan to centralize the schools and do away with the one he has, but is probably is a dead issue during the War. The meat is cheap and plenty, but is expected to run short by Christmas, too bad you can't freeze it - I have heard it can be kept fresh that way, but I think it takes electricity and that you don't have.

I have been to a Church fair in the Lutheran Church in Chatham last week. The Churches have to raise their own money to pay expenses and we pay 10 cent to get into the fair held in the Church basement. There were booths selling everything from clothing to cooking and candy. They had music and singing. Sometimes they put on dinners and you can get a nice one for 35 cents. When you go to Church here on Sunday mornings they have a couple of men going around with a dish collecting money so everyone is expected to put a little change in it - 5 to 10 cents - most pay 10 cents, so it is almost like paying for a ticket to go to Church.

Nothing new here. I go to work every morning and usually am free in the evening as Payn's hardly ever go anywhere at night, so I go next door to the Waltermire's and we talk or play cards.

Love to all

Hal

Saturday, Nov. 10, 1917

Dear all

I received your letters of Sept. 19 and Sept. 28 and you read in the papers again about US sending more men to Europe and drafting all aliens; it could be, but so far we have heard nothing here about it and the law has to be changed first before it can be done. I am getting tired of walking so I had a chance to buy an old Harley-Davidson motorcycle with side-car, so I use it to go up to Chatham and now I wish I had more time to use it, but now the winter is soon here and I can just store it till next summer.

I had a letter from the Bruens in New South Berlin and they asked me to come and visit them, but I can't go now, it is too far and the weather is too cold.

I hear the fuel is completely cut off to Denmark, so I am wondering how you get along, but I hope you can get some wood from Sweden.

The best to all

Hal

Sunday Evening, Dec.2, 1917

Dear all

Thanks for the letters from Oct. 10 - they usually take close to two months to get here. Glad Grandmother is feeling better again and can get out of bed. So you have no petroleum now, that is bad at this time of year when it gets dark at 3:30 p.m.. I am wondering how the farmers get their animals milked and fed in the dark or can you get candles?

You write again about the draft here, you must hear more about it than I do, but I asked Mr. Stupplebeen about it and he said they were going to take all men between the age of 19 and 42 and send nine million more over there, not counting the 100,000 already there, so that ought to put the Kaiser out of business. The men are going to be drafted after being enrolled in six categories. First volunteers and not married or no family dependents on them; second, people married, but with no children and so on. Number one goes first and they ship out as fast as they can get trained. This is just a proposal so far, but it will take time and I have to find out if I have to report change of address if I go South this winter.

You are asking me to come home, but there is no hurry yet and I probably couldn't get passage on a steamer now and what would I do in Denmark with no gasoline, petroleum, tires, no light and heat, rationing of bread, sugar, butter, margarine, meat and no work anywhere; and still I would not be home for Christmas. I hope you all get a Christmas present of the end of the War. It said here in the papers that Sweden was almost ready to jump in on Germany's side and if that happened Copenhagen would be taken and made a German U-boat harbor.

I have now been informed that we are going to North Carolina this winter to a city "Asheville" in the western part of the State in the Blue Mountains, not far from Tennessee, but 300 miles from the Atlantic Coast, and on the Southern slopes of the Allegheny Mountains - I don't know when we go, but it will be soon, so when you get this letter I may be there and I will be sunning myself between tobacco and cotton fields and enjoying the looks of the North Carolina girls; they tell me the women and girls there chew tobacco with the men. That is something, and they can spit tobacco juice as far as any man. I am enclosing my picture. I had to have some from the photographer for my 1918 chauffeurs license.

The best to all, Hal

Dec. 8, 1917
Chatham, New York

It is cold here now. Frost, down to 10 degree. days and zero at night, but no snow yet and I hope none comes before I get away from here. I have to drive the big limousine to Asheville, North Carolina. It is a city where many go in the wintertime. It is tucked in among the mountains and you can find it on your maps. I have collected some maps and have to find the place from the maps.

The new law about taking foreigners as draftees is coming up in Congress this winter, but it is planned to put them in Class no. 6 with married men with children, over 32, so everyone expects the war will be over before that. I am sending Adda some music for her piano. It is new war songs with music that is sung and played here everywhere. I also again sent that package of postcards from Bermuda that came back to me as the post office said packages couldn't be sent to Denmark. This time I sent them as letter mail and that cost me 42 cents where the package last summer cost 8 cents, but they told me it could go like that. I was in Albany last Thursday and bought a nice suit of clothes for $18, a pair of shoes for $5, rubbers for 65 cents and a suitcase for $10. My old suitcase was ready to fall apart. I also got a small bag for $7 made of leather, I needed it for the trip South, and it is the first time I spent that much money for clothes since I got here. I also got a hat for $1.50 and a wallet for $1 and that was plenty. I am ready to go so wish me luck.

Love to all and I will think of you on Christmas., Hal

December 17, 1917
Chatham

Dear all

No letters now in quite a while, so I expect a bunch of them when they get here. Too bad it takes so long for mail to go. We had a warmer day where the temperature almost hit 32 degrees during the day, then we had a snowstorm that lasted 24 hours and gave us 13 inches of snow that in some places blew up in drifts 24 to 30 inches high. So now I have something to look forward to going South. The trip is now suppose to start sometime between Christmas and New Years, but as usual, it can be changed over night.

Most everyone has a Christmas tree set up and decorated like we do and they look nice, also everywhere you hear people play Christmas carols.

I went to Dr. Walker, the dentist, to get my teeth fixed before leaving. He found two that needed attention. One got an ordinary filling, $1, but the other was a wisdom tooth and he put a gold crown on that for $5 - only it is so far back in my mouth so it doesn't show. That is too bad. I would like to show it off like the Americans do.

The new garage is nice to use in this weather as it is warm with central heating. It is built of red brick and holds three spaces for cars in the front part and a stable for six horses in the back wing.

Love to all

Hal

Dec. 30, 1917
Chatham

Dear all

As you can see I am still here. I got a letter from Soren and he said the ships - passenger liners - are not sailing anymore, so I don't know how the mail gets here, but I get letters even if they are two months on the way, but I hope they don't stop coming.

I was called to the draft board to be assigned a new class - as I am not over 31 and not married. I was put in class #5. That is still far down the list. The numbers go to Washington where the numbers are drawn in a lottery, but I understand they are still working on class #1. They are going to change the system when Congress starts to work in January, so will have to see what comes out.

We have a cold winter this year so early, and the temperature is still down to zero about every night and now I hear there is also snow in the Mountains of North Carolina, so that is not a place to go for a tan. The day of departure is now set for Tuesday, New Years Day, Jan. 1, and it looks like it is going to be a cold trip. Today it was close to zero all day and the wind is blowing some too, so when you go out it feels like you have no clothes on. Now I wish they would change our destination to Florida in place of North Carolina.

I have had a little cold for a few days, but that is gone. I was to Christmas dinner in the Church and a newspaper man was there and took a picture and all the names of the guests, so we were all in the paper, but everyone has trouble with my name - if they hear it they don't understand it, they can't spell it and if I spell it they can't read it. I hope you are all well and had a nice Christmas. I will continue my letters on my trip as soon and as often as I get time.

Love, Hal

CHAPTER NINE

The Trip South

Jan. 7, 1918
New York City

Dear all

As you can see, I am now finally in New York City on the way to the South. I left Chatham yesterday, Sunday Jan. 6, so you know the time was changed again from Jan. 1, but I am glad I am on the way, only at this time of the year you see no cars on the road as everyone has put them in storage for the winter, but we are different. Mr. and Mrs. Payn and their friend Mr. Hues left Chatham by train yesterday so I had a trip down here all by myself. I was sorry to say good-bye to my friends, the Waltermire's. Chatham is like my second home and the only one I have in this country, and everyone is nice and friendly. But, it is only for 3 to 4 months, then I will be back, I know these people were sorry to see me go as I could see they had tears in their eyes.

Now I am sitting here in the Athens Hotel located at 56 East 42nd Street, opposite New York Central and my first thought was to start writing letters to everyone. I had a tough ride here yesterday. The roads were very slippery and the snow was worked into ruts so you had to drive in the ruts and they were almost impossible to get out of again if I had to pass another car. The car would follow the rut like a streetcar on the track. I had to go slow and sometimes it would take 5 to 10 minutes for me or the other car to get out of the rut so we could pass sometimes on hills and I got the front wheels out of the ruts, the back wheels would refuse to come out and the car would slide sideways part way down a hill. One time it took 15 minutes to pass a car coming towards me in the same track. I had to stop and help push the car that the driver had managed to get sideways across the road so it was completely blocked. I finally got here last night and put the car in a garage and got a bed in this hotel and now I am going up to Mr. and Mrs. Payn to get my orders this afternoon and bring the car to the factory for a check before leaving on this long trip. It is raining and icing on the streets and accidents every few minutes when cars come together. When I get the car again I am ready to go, that means Wednesday Jan. 9.

Later

Mr. Payn is not going on the trip to Asheville with me. He and Mrs. Payn are going to take the train, but Mr. Hues is going with me. He is the man that lives in Malden Bridge and makes wooden pumps. He was in Bermuda for a while and did the milking when we had the cow. I like him and I am glad to have him with me so he will handle the expenses and we both keep our fingers crossed hoping the car can take it. I wish Mr. Payn had bought a Rolls Royce - nobody knows how to fix this car. I may not get a chance to write for a few days now, but I will as soon as I can.

Love to all

Hal

Jan. 17, 1918
Asheville, North Carolina

Dear all

As you see I am now in Asheville, North Carolina after an interesting, but strenuous trip. It is unbelievable the States can keep their roads in such bad condition. But I will start from the beginning:

I came to New York City on Sunday, Jan. 6. Monday and Tuesday I had the Owen-Magnetic car to the factory for a complete check-up before leaving, and Wednesday morning, 9 a.m., I left New York City. It was a freezing rainstorm and I had chains on all four wheels to help me get out of the ruts. The streets were very slippery and everywhere I saw fender bumpers going at it on the streetcars when they tried to stop and couldn't.

Mr. Hues was with me sitting inside in the back seat. I was hoping for better weather as we got further South. New York had some snow, but it was mostly melted now and as the day got warmer I expected it to disappear. The first four hours got us a few miles down in New Jersey and the snow on the ground got heavier, and we soon had three feet of snow, but the main State road was shoveled out some places. The road was only passable for one car at a time and every 1/2 mile or so it was wide enough for two cars so that was where I would have to wait for traffic going the opposite way.

The road was straight and I could see for miles, but the road was lower than the fields, so the snow had drifted in and filled it. Now with the snow half melted I found 1/2 foot of water in the tracks where there was no snow and other places I just had the ruts to follow, you got into them and could not get out of them again when you wanted to.

It is 106 miles from New York to Philadelphia, and under normal conditions it is a four hour drive, but it took us all day and we were beginning to worry about getting there before dark, as we easily could get on a wrong road and get lost, so we never stopped until I got so tired and hungry I just had to rest for a while. So we came to a little village at 3 p.m. and stopped there for a cup of coffee and a sandwich. They told us we still had 30 miles to Philadelphia and not to expect better driving. We had to go on and after about ten miles the road seemed to get a little better, and after another ten miles the snow was all gone and we had a fair to good blacktop road ahead of us and we now could get to Philadelphia fast.

In Philadelphia we were told they had no snow this winter and they were amazed to hear there was three feet of snow on the ground only thirty miles North of here. We went looking for a hotel and the only one we could get a room in only had this one room with two double beds, so Mr. Hues and I had a room together, but we each had a big bed.

We were there as it was getting dark, the car was in a garage, where it could be made ready for the next morning, and we had our dinner and soon went to bed. We didn't feel like doing any sightseeing, and we slept good until 6:30 a.m..

Thursday Jan. 10, we wanted to get an early start, so we had our breakfast as soon as we could get it, and were ready to start at 8 a.m.; we would like to reach Washington today as we expect better roads, and it is 104 miles to Baltimore and 38 more to Washington - total 142 miles. When we got outside Philadelphia, we found a wide blacktop road, but it was very worn and full of holes filled with water, but no trace of snow. We had to go slow, but could keep a steady pace, so after ten miles of that I stopped and took all the chains off the wheels as they had started to wear, and everything looked better.

The sun was shining and even with a little frost in the shade the sun felt good. Yesterday Mr. Hues had complained about it being cold inside the back of the car and my front compartment was cold too, but today, with the sun out it was comfortable. I get some heat from the motor, and then the sun made us feel the South was getting close.

Another twenty miles and we got into a section that had more ice on the road and fields, but it was melting in the sun, so we expected that to be better as the sun got warmer and it did get better on the South side of the hills, but still bad on the North side.

We kept going steadily and reached Baltimore after six hours steady driving, at 2 p.m. We stopped for lunch and a rest. We had to ask for a place to get gasoline and then filled the tanks. Outside Baltimore, the road was new and blacktop and had no holes; the sun was now warmer and most places the ice was melted off the road. We met 50 army trucks, all brand new, going North and we pulled over and stopped for them and took another breather.

We got to Washington DC, shortly after 4 p.m. Again we had a little trouble finding hotel rooms, so to save time we took one room together, two beds, and it was nice. It cost four dollars for two persons. We had dinner in the hotel. Mr. Hues had the expense money, so he took care of everything and I was glad I had him along.

We knew Washington would be the last outpost of the North and we would have unknown and almost uncharted traveling from here on. We knew there would be roads and we also knew they would be bad, but so far, so good. I took time after the dinner to go for a long walk. I saw the Capitol and the White House where the President lives.

The beds were calling and I was tired so we soon turned in, we were aiming for Richmond, Virginia, as the target for the next day - 134 miles.

This is the end of Thursday, Jan. 10, our second day out of New York. Friday Jan. 11, we got out of bed early, had breakfast and got the car and was on our way after a little trouble finding the right road out of Washington. The road looked good. The weather was cold and a light frost; we knew we would hit bad roads, but this was a nice blacktop road, so we made good time for about thirty miles, then the blacktop ended, but the road continued and we saw a rutted, red clay road leading across a swamp and it was just wide enough for one car. I saw two deep ruts for the wheels and I was wondering how you could pass anybody, but I saw no one else, so we were the only ones that were foolish enough to drive that road. It was just passable for mules pulling carts, but we had no choice but to try it, so we went in. As luck was with us, the road was frozen so we didn't sink in, but we had to stay in the ruts as they were so deep it was impossible to get out of them.

The swamp was flat land with water and ice swimming around and also trees that got dense as we drove on - we didn't see anybody else for miles until we came to a little village. There the woods ended and the road was just as bad through the village.

I stopped for a cup of coffee and we found out the road would be getting better but with some hills, so I had the chains put on the wheels again as the sun now was melting the frozen surface. We continued again and still had the same road, until we got to a place where the water had run across the road and made a gully about 24 inches wide and full of water, still running like a creek. I put on a little speed so as not to be stalled in it and, to my surprise, it was about 12 inches deep and the front wheels fell into it and jumped out again, almost upsetting the car. I then jumped the back wheels in and out and I was happy I didn't get stuck there. On the other side I stopped and took a look at the wheels and springs, but everything was all right.

We continued toward Richmond, Virginia. The roads didn't get any better, but started to freeze and that helped some. After a while we started to see snow on the fields and we soon were driving through four inches of snow. Later in the afternoon, it started to snow harder and we got to Richmond in a snowstorm at 5 p.m. We only saw a few villages and mostly woods all the way from Washington. We found a hotel, got the car in a garage to be cleaned and serviced, had a good dinner. Mr. Hues wanted to rest and I went to the movies. Before I went back to the hotel to go to bed the snow had turned to rain.

That was the end of our 3rd day, Friday, the 11th.

Saturday Jan. 12 was planned to be our longest ride to the next city of Durham in North Carolina, 175 miles from Richmond. It has been a difficult trip so far, but even if it is difficult and we get exhausted, I pick up strength fast when I get my dinner at night, and we feel like explorers, as we get told no one was ever passing that way from the North at this time of year. We were told that the first 22 miles from Richmond to Petersburg would be very bad, after that we would find better going, so we started out early again, hoping to make it to Durham before dark, as we would rather not stop over in a small village, most of them without a hotel or even a garage where we could buy gasoline.

I had the chains fixed and put on the rear wheels so we could pull through the red clay and mud, and they were not kidding when they said the road was bad - it was the worst I have ever seen. It was a main State road and probably good in the summertime, it was wide enough for two or even three cars, but it went through a country of that red clay, and it looked like there were no stones or even gravel as we know it in the North. There was just no bottom to these ruts, and the road was just built up with red clay dug out of the ditches on the sides and thrown in the middle of the road.

We soon passed two big trucks stuck in the clay halfway up a small hill, they had sunk down in the clay right to the axles and the steps, and the rain from last night had made it worse, so we were hoping for a freeze to tighten things up, but that was out for here. We went slowly but did not stop as we were afraid we would not be able to get started again. We drove for several hours and saw only a few houses and very few small villages with just a few houses on each side of the road. The trees were mostly pines trees, but nothing else was green. Everything seems to be covered with this red clay as was our car and my shoes, by this time.

Slowly, after about 75 miles or so, the road seemed to get more solid, but still far from good. Petersburg was behind us , but we could see no end to this miserable State road. We don't even think about what would happen if we get stalled ten miles or more from nowhere.

While the roads now were less greasy, they were now full of deep holes and ruts. It is a wonder Mr. Hues, sitting in the back seat, could keep his head on straight, as he was hitting the ceiling in the cab every time we hit a hole. He kept his heavy felt hat on to protect his head. I could not slow down too much now as it didn't look like we were going to make it to Durham before dark.

About 1 p.m. after 5 1/2 hours on the road we needed a rest, and we had covered half of the distance. We could see it would be 8 p.m. and long after dark before we would be in Durham, but we may try it as the road is easy to follow on this stretch. The telephone poles on our route are marked, one blue and two white stripes, and by following this marking we will end up in Durham, North Carolina.

So, we made this stop at 1 p.m., in a very small village by the name of South Hill, to get our lunch. Some Negroes were hanging around the corner near where we stopped and they came over to look at us and the car, and then one of them said "It looks to me like you are about to lose your spare tires, but maybe that is the way it is suppose to be". The tires and wheels were on the back of the car in a carrier and it was true, the rack had broken and the tires were hanging down in the back of the car, and dragging in the mud. I had two spare tires and wheels there, and the shaking from driving over the holes had broken the bolts and bent the rods holding the rack to the back of the car, and the weight had bent the entire rack down.

As luck would be there was a garage and machine shop in this town and they promised to start to fix it right away, so we left the car there while we ate lunch. We waited three hours and then the car was again ready to go. The sun was now out and felt warm in the sun and we felt we had left the snow and ice and frost behind and now things were looking up. Durham was now out of the question for tonight and we said we would settle for a stop in Oxford, 25 miles short of Durham. We went on and it got dark and cold. The ground was now again partly frozen and it looked like we again were in a colder climate.

We went through another small town and now were 22 miles from Oxford. The road was now frozen and that was a help as it was getting much more rutted and we were driving in the ruts made by wagons. We could only drive very slow and we finally got to Oxford, North Carolina at 8 p.m. We stopped at a hotel, It was the only one. It was the Hotel Oxford. We complained about the roads and they told us they were no better for the next 25 miles, into Durham. The hotel was the dirtiest hotel I have ever seen. They had all nigger help, and the white people I saw did nothing, but order the blacks around.

Virginia and South Carolina are dry States - that means no alcohol is sold, and this town was dry all right - we could not even get a glass of water. The landlord said all the water pipes in the village were frozen and they didn't know if we could get any gasoline, but we could try in the General Store. The place was cold and there was only a fireplace to heat the building.

A nigger was trying to get the fire going with a few pieces of wood and a few people were crowding around the fireplace to get a little of the heat. Our rooms were two dollars for each and they demanded us to pay in advance. We wanted to get an early start in the morning, so I tried to buy gasoline before dinner that evening and they had some in a drum at the store. They filled my tank with a pail and a funnel. Then I had to drain the water out of the radiator so it would not freeze, as we had to leave the car outside overnight. We saved the water to use it in the morning.

After a bad dinner we went to bed to get an early start in the morning, as we wanted to make up for the 25 miles to Durham, plus next day's scheduled trip - Durham to Charlotte, North Carolina - a total of 150 miles. Oxford is a nice town if you have plenty of time, but we were up at 7 a.m. and when we went down to the dining room we saw the owner sitting in a big rocking chair in front of the fireplace and he was scolding a young nigger boy because he didn't move fast enough and get the fire going hotter so the house would get warm. He made no effort to get out of the chair himself.

We asked to get some water to wash in, and he said "sure, just give us a little time till some more of the help shows up, then we will get water and breakfast". We sat down and waited and at 8:30 a.m., we got a water pitcher with some lukewarm water; we took it upstairs and got cleaned up, and soon we were down again and waited some more for breakfast. That we got at 9:30 a.m. and it took one hour for eggs, bacon and a cup of something that didn't taste much like coffee. Then I went out and got the car's motor going and put water in the radiator. But there was not enough water and we couldn't get anymore, so we drove off anyway and got some water from someone that had a pump on the outskirts of town. We were on the way now.

The road was frozen and it was our fifth day out of New York, and it was Sunday Jan. 13. We went slowly. The ruts were cutting our tires and we soon came to a place where the road went right down into a creek, and we had to drive across it and up the other side, 20 yards across, with the water up to the middle of the wheels, but it gave us no trouble. We soon came to another creek with the same arrangement. They don't believe in spending money for bridges here. This creek was also full of floating pieces of ice. We couldn't make it to Charlotte, but had to stop for the night in Greensboro, but we were slowly getting to the end of our first part of this trip to Asheville. If we were lucky, another day would bring us there and I think we were lucky to get this far without any serious trouble.

Next day was Monday Jan. 14, our sixth day on the road, and we got an early start from Greensboro. Yesterday we had a little snow on the fields, but now there was no snow, but the roads were still bad, and it was two p.m. before we reached Charlotte, North Carolina and another 124 miles would bring us to Asheville. But it was now 2 p.m. so we knew we could not make it, but another day didn't make that much difference, so we picked a place on the map that looked promising. It was King Mountain, only 88 miles from Asheville, but we almost didn't get there. We went through Charlotte and about 12 miles out, we came to a river that had a long toll bridge over it. The bridge was damaged during the night, and had collapsed in the center where the roadway had sunk down so the water was just lapping over it. The toll collector told us we could go over it if we wanted to, he thought it may hold up, but we wanted none of that.

Several horse and mule drawn wagons were also stranded there, and someone said there was another bridge some 25 miles up the river where we could cross, but we had to go back to Charlotte and take another road. We didn't like the delay and extra miles, but at least we could do it; but the people stranded there with their wagons were out of luck - it was too far for them to go.

We took the advice and went back to Charlotte, found the other road and the other bridge and got to King's Mountain by 6 p.m., only 88 miles from Asheville, over Rutherfordton and Chimney Rock. That was Monday Jan. 14, and we were glad to be so close to the end of the trip. We found a hotel. It was really bad, but we had no choice, and we got the car in a garage where they fixed the chains that we still had to use; and we were told the road to Asheville over the mountains was impassable now in the wintertime and we would have to go South to Spartanburg in South Carolina and that way bypass the steepest part of the mountains. Tomorrow will be our seventh day on the road and hopefully the last.

We have been able to see the Mountains in a haze in the West for the last couple of days. We have not seen any blacktop roads since leaving, I think, a few miles south of Washington, and I am beginning to think the whole South is a great big mess of mud.

Tuesday Jan. 15, we pulled out of Kings Mountain and with no trouble we reached Spartanburg, where we stopped for lunch. Spartanburg is now, since the war, a big Army base and we saw a lot of Army trucks and soldiers. We have seen no cars on the road since leaving Petersburg, Virginia, and just a few trucks and most of them stalled in the mud. We were still driving in that red clay and these roads were cut up more by the traffic from the Army Base where they had to use mostly mules for transportation. The road had ruts 12 to 18 inches deep, filled with water. One place we hit had a deep hole in one rut and when we hit that, the car went over on two wheels and the dirty water sprayed over the car like a waterfall. I was thinking the car would turn over, but it righted itself again, but I could not see a thing as the windshield was covered with dirty water running off the roof. It was like driving on the bottom of the ocean and all I could do was try to keep the car going straight as the ditches on the side were two or three yards deep.

We came out of that and went a few more miles out of Spartanburg, towards the Mountain. We came to a place where the road was lower than the fields on the sides and it was just one big lake. It was near the Army Base, and there was a string of carts, each pulled by six mules. The carts were filled with bales of hay and one soldier was sitting on each mule. That must have been the best way to do it there, as we saw a big truck stalled in the mud, in the center of that lake. They had a lot of mules pulling on it there in the water, trying to get that truckload of hay out of there.

We had to get across there too, and plunged in and everybody stopped working too look at us, expecting us to get stuck, but we must by luck have picked a better place. We went in till the water and mud covered the running boards and was over the axles. I was afraid the water would get in the motor, but we kept going and slowly came out on the other side, and slowly pulled away on our way towards the mountains ahead.

It was a beautiful day, the sun was out and felt warm, but the Mountains (The Blue Mountains) ahead we could see now were covered with snow, and we had to get over them to reach Asheville on the other side. We kept going until we reached the foot of the mountains, so close we had to lay our heads back to see the top and it didn't look good. The road we were on stopped by a broken bridge over a wide creek; that bridge about 50 feet across must have been broken a long time, and I could see the tracks where mules and wagons had crossed through the water down over the bank and up the other on the far side. Mr. Hues came out of the car when I stopped, (most of the time I forgot about him being in there) and we looked at the bridge, but we couldn't use it so we walked down the slope to the water. The water was running fast, but the banks looked like they were mostly gravel and not that soft clay we had been driving in, and the other side was not steep, so we decided to take a chance on crossing. We could see a house about 1/2 mile up the road on the other side, and we could see the road climbing up and up higher on the side of the mountain.

We got in and swung down the bank and in the water that was almost up to the doors for a minute, but we hit some boulders under the water and the front wheels went over them and when they came down on them, the bottom of the motor hit something and I heard the crash, but we moved forward and the rear wheels went over the boulders and then we came out and up the bank to the road on the other side. I stopped and looked under the car and it looked like I had a big dent in the oil pan under the motor. We couldn't do anything about that, and the motor was working perfectly, so we continued up the mountain road.

It was getting narrow now, most of the time for just one car and here and there a passing place. We came to a very small settlement and asked them there about the road, and they told us no car had been over that road since last summer, and they didn't think we could make it, and also that it was nine miles to the top where we would get to a little village. The road clung to the side of the Mountain, one curve after another. At times the road was just cut in the side of a steep rock wall, and we could see a few houses down in the valley, straight down 300 to 400 feet and the mountain wall straight up over our heads to the top.

The road was now icy and had about one foot of snow on it almost turned to ice, but there was the track of a mule cart, the ruts it had made, and we drove in that track with the chains biting in the ice. At places the cliff was so close to the track that I would not have been able to open the door and get out without tumbling down to the valley below. It was impossible to turn back, so we kept going up, up and up. The landscape turned into winter, the road twisted and turned, and at times we could see the road we traveled over a half hour ago down below us. The snow covered ditches and we had to depend on the ruts to show us the way. We came to a place where the water had run down the side of the cliff, run over the road, an on down the other side - it was a real slide there for about two or three feet - and on the whole trip up that mountain, or anywhere else for that matter, did we see any handrails.

That ice slide disappeared over the side of the road straight down to the valley several hundred feet below, but we could see the wheels from the cars had made a slight indentation in the ice. I thought the chains would hold the car, but Mr. Hues for the first time said he would walk across and get in if I made it to the other side. He walked ahead and I got in and kept the car at a steady speed across the ice. When the front wheels were over I knew the rear would go too with the chains on them to hold. After that, Mr. Hues got in and we went on for another couple of miles.

We came to a place where the road had slid out and disappeared in the valley below. But the tracks had left the road there and went up close to the cliff across the ditch and there was just room enough to get the car through between the cliff wall and the hole that had slid out and down in the car. This time Mr. Hues stayed. We watched the speedometer and knew we were getting near the top, but it was also getting late in the afternoon. We had to pass over a few small bridges where some of the boards that made the roadway were missing and then we came to a place where a rockslide had left some rocks in the road. Just two of the rocks were too big for the car to go over, so I took a chain I had in the toolbox and tied it around the rocks and the other end to the front side of the car. By backing up I broke the rock loose where they were frozen in the snow, and Mr. Hues and I rolled them over on the side. We were now almost to the top and the road was getting better, and not too steep and a little wider too, when we were stopped again. A tree was laying across the road and it was frozen fast so it must have been there for some time.

Mr. Hues and I tried to move it, but couldn't, so I got the chain out again and soon had the tree loose and pulled it along the road as I backed the car up. Now we could roll it over on the side so we could get by. We were now soon up on the flat land on top of the mountain and we got to a little village, Saluda, and it was 5:30 p.m. and dark. We didn't want any more mountain road that day, so we asked a man for a hotel or lodging and food. He said there was no hotel or diner, but we could stop and talk with the sheriff in that house over there.

We did that and he said we could stay with him if we wanted and he had enough for us to eat supper with him, so we left the car in front of his house and I had to drain the water out of the radiator. He wanted to know how we got there and he couldn't believe us, he said no car had ever before taken that trip in the wintertime - it was considered impossible. Well, I was just a dumb Dane and didn't know it couldn't be done.

We called Mr. Payn at his hotel in Asheville and told him where we were and that we would be seeing him the next day. He said he had expected us a couple of days ago and had begun to worry about us. That was the end of our trip for Tuesday Jan. 15, our seventh day of travel.

Main state highway in N.C.

Wednesday Jan. 16, 1918

Just one week ago we left New York, and if I had known what a trip that was going to be I may have quit right then; and then again who knows . I seem to thrive on it. We slept good, had a nice breakfast and I got out and readied the car. Put water in the radiator, I took a look at the oil in the motor, and it was very low and I could see a puddle of oil under the car, so I was sure we had a crack in the oil pan where we put that dent yesterday. "There was a place down the road where we could get gas and oil." said the sheriff, so we put our bags in the car and bid the sheriff and his wife good-bye. The motor started easily and I got in and tried to drive, but the car would not move. I found out then that the brake bands had frozen fast to the brake drums overnight. There was some snow on the ground and it was cold and freezing.

I had to ask the sheriff for a pail of hot water and got that after a while. I poured that over the wheels and brake drums; that loosened them and now we were off, we stopped and got gas and all the oil the motor could take. We had about 1/2 hour driving on the same kind of mountain road, now going down, but then the road flattened out and got good except for a layer of snow. We got to Asheville shortly after noon and had driven 900 miles in 7 1/2 days. That was a poor record, but under those conditions it was excellent.

It is still freezing and cold here, and I have no car, it is being repaired in the nearby garage. The oil pan had to be taken off and welded, but outside of that the car just needed a good cleaning inside and out. I didn't think a car could hold up the way this car did, and I think our lives depended on that car more than once.

"The Great Room" Grove Park Inn, Asheville, N.C.

The hotel, Grove Park Inn is on a little hill, overlooking the Blue Ridge Mountains and the city of Asheville. It is a summer resort, but now it is winter here and everything is covered with snow. Mr. and Mrs. Payn said today it was too cold to stay here and they were just spending a few days here, then we would go to Florida. We are going for rides in the mountains here, but staying on the good roads no more than five miles from the city. This was a long letter, but it was a long ride - so love to you all

Hal

Sunday, Jan. 20, 1918

It is a beautiful countryside here and I would like to see it in the summertime, but now it is out of season and there are just a few tourists here. The hotel is only 1/2 mile out of Asheville on a little hill, and it is an exclusive place and very expensive.

The big lobby as you enter the building has a mammoth fireplace that is said to be the biggest in the world. All the walls and pillars are built up with local granite as is the fireplace, and the guests can sit there in wicker chairs and overlook the lawn and the city below through a big expanse of glass. There is a garage in the back near the entrance road. I have my room upstairs there and eat in a small dining room in the hotel. In this weather there is not much you can do, and Mr. and Mrs. Payn, Mr. Hues and some friends they have here are usually sitting in the lobby, and they are ready to go to Florida any time now. Mr. Hues and I are going to drive there in the car, but Mr. and Mrs. Payn are taking the train. We will be leaving Wed. Jan. 23 and our destinations will be Ormond Beach, just north of Daytona Beach.

Love to all of you.

Hal

Jan 27, 1918
Savannah

Dear all

Just before leaving Asheville, North Carolina, I got a lot of letters from Denmark, including some sent here by Mr. Stupplebeen. They came to Chatham after I left and he is also going to see that I get my letters when I get to Florida. I see Dad is still not feeling too good and now with the winter coming it is bad to be sick. I sure hope you are all well by now. I wish I could send you some of the nice weather we have here in Georgia, where we are stopping on our way to Florida.

We had a real tough time getting here, those miserable roads are still with us so far. But from here it should get better. Here is how it went :

We left Asheville on Wednesday, the 23rd, after a week there, and we didn't have really too bad roads, but it was snowing. We had to get over the Mountains again, this time heading for Greenville, South Carolina. It was a better road than the one we came here on. It went up and around the mountain in hairpin curves along cliffs and over bridges, but it was better although there were no guardrails. We had 4-5 inches of snow on the road in most places, but where the sun had been able to get at it, it was melted down to the bare road in the tracks. Someone must have worked on this road, and after a while we saw who it was. Just before coming to Greenville, we saw a bunch of prisoners in striped uniforms working on the road and the guards were standing near with guns trained on them. We didn't stop to look, but went in to Greenville where we expected to stay.

It was only 3 p.m., and after a sandwich and a cup of coffee, we continued for another couple of hours to a little town, Ware Shoal, where we saw a big cotton mill. In South Carolina the farmers raise mostly cotton and we meet them with loads of cotton bales going to town. The bales are pressed and covered with a cloth and have iron bands holding them together.

We still had snow in Ware Shoal and we found a fair hotel and got an early start the next morning going toward Augusta on the way to the coast. We thought it would be about 75 miles to there, only we got bad news at the garage when we picked up the car in the morning. We asked about the road to Augusta and they told us an officer from the Army Base in Spartanburg had come in the garage a few days ago and said he came from Augusta and it had taken him three days to get to Ware Shoal over that road. His little two-passenger car had been unable to negotiate the road and he had to hire mules and oxen to pull him and his car most of the way.

There was no bottom to the ruts in that road, and our best bet would be to just drive when the road was frozen like it was just now. We had the chains put on the rear wheels; I had four chains when we left New York, but one was lost somewhere, so I now had three; that gave me one extra chain in case I lost another.

We made 18 miles before the road started to get real soft from the warmer air towards noon, and the car sunk in the ruts so I could only move in second gear as the wheels were pushing the mud aside, as the ruts didn't seem to fit the width of the track the car made. We could only go 5-8 m.p.h. and in the center of a woods we stalled on a hill. One of the wheels started to spin in the greasy mud. I had to get out in the mud and walk back to look. One of the chains had broken and was missing, so in all that mud I had to jack up my wheel and put on my last chain. I got that done and we were again on our way, but the motor began to heat up and the water boiled in the radiator. So I stopped again and shut the motor off so it would cool off. The radiator was completely plugged up so the fan could not draw any air through it to cool it. The mud had splattered up on it and also the motor was covered with mud. When I went to use the hand crank to start the motor again I found the crank slightly bent from plowing through the mud. I straightened it somewhat, and after one hours work we got it going and were again on the way in second gear.

Soon the motor stopped again. I got it started again and we made another couple of miles; then the radiator was boiling and the car looked like a locomotive with the steam coming out, so we stopped again. I tried to get some water out of the ditch along the road, and filled the radiator with dirty water. It helped a little for a while and we moved forward again.

We stopped, we started, we moved a little forward; stop, start, stop, start, move a little and we got out of the woods and could see a farmhouse ahead, before we got there the car stopped again and this time we had again lost a chain. I had no more chains so I started to walk back in the track of the car to look for the broken chain. We had had nothing to eat or drink all day since 7 a.m. and now it was 4 p.m. and I had a headache and felt sick. Mr. Hues walked ahead to the farm. I had put on the rubber boots and the mud and clay stuck to my boots so my feet felt like they were 100 pounds each.

I had to walk back about one mile to find the chain. I walked back to the farm and got some tools and repaired the chain while a bunch of Negroes stood around watching, then I had to jack the car up and put the chain back on and now I could drive it into the farmer's driveway. By then it was 6 p.m., and Mr. Hues had made a deal with the farmer for us to stay overnight. I was getting to feel worse and my head ached, so after we got washed up and had some supper, Mr. Hues took my temperature and I had 100 degrees, so I knew I had a touch of the influenza. We went to bed after I had taken some pills, but in the morning I didn't feel much better. The farmer said it was 30 miles to Augusta, but we would find the road much better after about five miles driving. This was now Friday the 25th, and we started out again after a good breakfast. I had cleaned some of the mud out of the radiator and it was filled with water. We went about five miles in second gear and then the road got more sandy and not so muddy and we made it in to Augusta, 20 miles, that morning.

I still didn't feel good so we got the car in the garage and Mr. Hues wanted me to go to a doctor, but by then I seemed a little better and we had a light lunch and we decided to stay there and get the car fixed, and get a good rest. In the hotel room Mr. Hues again took my temperature and it was almost down to normal. I had a nosebleed that afternoon and Mr. Hues got concerned again, but I had a good appetite for dinner.

We had a room together again here in Augusta, and I got some Quinine pills I took and went to bed. Mr. Hues tucked me in and I slept good all night and was O.K. in the morning, only a little tired.

On Saturday, the 26th, at Augusta, Georgia we realized we were in the South and it now looked like we were finished with ice and snow and mud. We started on the road to Savannah on the coast and the sun was out warm and nice and the roads were now getting more sandy and dry as the water could drain off or down, wherever water goes. We went through big woods of mostly pine trees, and we had some blacktop streets in Augusta, but outside the city line the road was sandy, but at least not wet, and the motor worked good so we made good time.

We saw some oxen pulling wagons loaded with big loads of pine logs and when we got to about 20 miles from Savannah, we saw our first palm tree and soon more of them. They look kind of scrawny like the frost had been too hard on them, and we saw a lot of other trees still without leaves, but the grass was green and the small bushes were also green in the gardens where they are tended - some places the grass was burned off by the sun in the hot summer and it had not started to grow yet. An unusual amount of fires were visible in the woods where it was burning in the grass among the trees and the smoke was drifting across the road. The trees were getting covered with moss hanging down from the branches and that amazed me and gave the trees a ghostly look, as the moss is gray and long and even grows out along the telephone wires. It was a beautiful and for me, an unusual sight. Mr. Hues and I arrived in Savannah early in the afternoon and we were surprised to find Mr. and Mrs. Payn here too. They found the place so delightful, they decided to stay a few days and Mr. Hues and I can stand a few days rest too, and a chance to see the city.

Love to all

Hal

Friday, February 1, 1918

We left Savannah and headed for Jacksonville, Florida. Mr. Hues and I are both looking forward to get to Florida - the land of sunshine and alligators. We got started at 8 a.m. and we each carried a package of sandwiches. We never before thought to bring anything to eat, and it usually ended up with us driving all day without eating, but that wasn't going to happen to us today.

The road was narrow and sandy and it passed through long stretches of woods on land covered with water, and little islands of dry land here and there. The trees were covered with that hanging moss, and we didn't see any farms or much traffic except a couple of oxen teams. After three hours driving we came to a broad river (St. George River) that forms the border between Georgia and Florida, but there was no bridge except a railroad bridge, so we had to backtrack a few miles to a railroad station where we got the car on a flatcar and then we had to wait for a train to come and transport us and the car over the river. We only had to wait one hour so we were lucky. It was six miles till the next station on the Florida side of the river, where we got put on a sidetrack and got unloaded. On the train we ate our sandwiches and we were glad we had them. With us on the train was another car from New York City, a really sporty looking two-passenger car. The man driving it said he and the car came by ship to Savannah as the roads were impassable from Washington to Savannah. Now we were on our wheels again and the sports car soon was out of sight. About one hour later we came to another river, but this had a small ferry. The ferry was now on the opposite side and we could see our friend in the sports car driving off the ferry. We waited for the ferry to come over and take us across. The small ferry was just big enough to hold one car and that seemed to overload it.

It was now 4 p.m., and we estimated our New York friend was 15 minutes ahead of us. We talked to the ferry man and he said about ten miles ahead we would get to the little village of Yulee, and we had better inquire there about a bridge near Jacksonville that was broken down, it may not be passable.

We got to Yulee and were told the bridge was not repaired and could not be used. Jacksonville was 15 miles away over that bridge, but we would have to go 45 miles to bypass that bridge. Mr. Hues said our luck has run out for today, better luck tomorrow, but we will go as far as we can. We were told the roads were bad and now it was 5 p.m., but we did what we had done now for three weeks - we continued ahead. The road soon got to be just two tracks through the woods and sometimes the road disappeared entirely and we could see several tracks in and out between the trees. Everyone passing had picked their own way between the trees. We came to a stream and it was very muddy and looked deep. I stopped and got a tree branch to see how deep it was and I could see three places where someone had crossed it, but that could have been wagons trying first one place and then another and a third, and all three looked like mud holes.

While we were there, our friend from New York drove up. He said he didn't stop in Yulee, but continued toward Jacksonville and got to the downed bridge and he had to go back, that is how he got behind us. He was a hot shot and he gunned his motor and put on some speed that he thought would take him across the stream. He sunk in the middle of the hole where he hit a tree stump. He tried to back up, but his wheels only dug in more and soon we couldn't even see his wheels.

Well, I took my shoes and socks off and went out to him. He had a rope in his car and I had a long chain so we got him out of the hole. We were all wet so we examined the next hole and waded across it - it looked more promising so I was going to try that, but first I jacked the wheels up and put my snow chains on; he did the same on his car and now I drove out in the hole with him watching. If I got stuck he would pull me out, but I got across; now it was his turn and he also made it, so now he was not in a hurry anymore, and he suggested we stay together until the road got better. It was now 6 p.m. and getting dark, and it looked like we were lost in the woods as we could see no road. We drove a short distance between the trees and then we saw a boy and asked him for directions. He said we were on a lumber trail and had missed a turn somewhere back so we would have to go back through the mud holes. We turned around and after passing through the mud holes we found the right road. It soon got better and after three hours of driving we got to Jacksonville at 9 p.m. We were exhausted and found a place to stay, then dinner and bed.

Owen-Magnetic stuck on Georgia clay road

Saturday, February 22, 1918

Jacksonville is now past us. We got off early and again brought a sandwich with us. We had 120 miles to Ormond Beach, but we were not taking any chances on eats. We were heading South leaving Jacksonville, we had to cross a river on a ferry (St. John's River) and we now had a nice brick paved road along the ocean for about ten miles, then the road got narrow and very sandy and it went into the woods so dense even a bird couldn't fly here it seems. In Florida we had to change our watches and set them ahead one hour. The road got more like ruts in the sand and we had to cross numerous bridges and they were all in bad repair. They had loose heavy planks for driveway and sometimes one plank would be missing here and there, leaving holes 12 inches wide we had to drive over.

We got out of the woods and soon saw big fruit farms with orange trees and the sun was out and it was warm summer when we got to Ormond Beach. Mr. Payn was there to meet us at the big hotel (Ormond Hotel) near the river that parallels the beach. The hotel had a big garage where a lot of cars were kept, all belonging to the guests. There were also acres of golf courses. I was sent to a guesthouse across the road from the hotel, where I had a nice room and also got my board. We found out about the beach, that the cars could drive on it for about 20 miles going South where the sand was wet and hard so the wheels didn't sink in one bit; it is flat and smooth like driving on a floor, but only at low tide. When the tide is in and the water covers the beach you better not try it. Cars caught there at high tide are ruined by salt water.

The well known millionaire John D. Rockefeller spends his winter here in the same hotel where Mr. and Mrs. Payn are staying and he always has a pocketful of dimes that he uses for tips, never more than one dime and never less. Mr. and Mrs. Payn don't play golf, but like to go there and watch and one day John D. Rockefeller was with us. He is old and doesn't play either, but I got one of his dimes as a tip when we got back to the hotel.

The war is getting more serious everyday now and we are beginning to feel it more, but still not as bad as it is in Denmark. We now have meatless days, and wheatless days, where we eat bread made from corn or rye. Also, all factories are now closed on Mondays to save fuel and that goes for most private stores too. It is not bad compared to what you have, but I hear it is bad in New York where they don't have enough coal and it now is below zero temperature there. They have also changed the time one hour to save fuel for light, so I heard it was not only here in Florida that was done. I am going to start taking some pictures here as I can get many beautiful shots here. I hope we stay here till the weather gets good in New York.

Love to all

Hal

**February 25, 1918
Ormond Beach Florida**

Dear Mom and Dad.

I just received your letter sent at Christmas, so that took two months to get here. I am happy Adda and Soren now are married and have a flat to move into; that is they will be married by the time this letter gets to Denmark. Too bad that war causes shortages of just about everything and a lot of people are out of work in Denmark. Here is a shortage of workmen and now they are paying $20.00 to $25.00 and sometimes $30.00 a week for help in the factories. Here time is moving slow and I am getting tired of the same thing every day. We take a trip down the beach in the car about every forenoon from 10 a.m. to 12 noon, and I get up at 7 a.m., get ready for breakfast 7:30 and shortly after 8 a.m. I am in the garage across the street along side the hotel where I wash the car. It gets very dusty here from the sand, so it is always shining when we go out.

We go the 1/2 mile to the beach and then drive on the beach if the tide is out and the water low. Here from Ormond Beach we can drive 18 miles South to the inlet to Halifax River, going North we can only drive a couple of miles, then the sand gets soft and some places there is quicksand where a car can sink in and eventually disappear so we never go North on the beach; some do if they don't know the risk.

I just heard a man from the North came here and rented a car in Daytona, an Overland, and the first trip he took was up the beach. He could feel the sand getting soft under the car and tried to turn around, but when he slowed down for the turn he started to sink and soon stalled, unable to move. That was late in the afternoon and only two hours before the tide would bring the water in and over the spot where he was stuck. He left the car and went to a nearby house to telephone for help, but before help came the wheels were out of sight. Now it took four hours work in the water to get the car out and the water was over the motor, so I think that car was ruined.

All iron and steel rusts here in the salt air and sand. About three miles South on the beach we get to Daytona Beach and there is a man with two airplanes that does passenger flying over the water and city. He charges ten dollars for ten minutes and takes off and lands on the beach where all the cars are driving. One day we were pulled up on the side watching him take off and land, and he came down right over a moving car and ripped the top of the car with his tailskid and the windshield was shattered. The people in the car got a couple of clunks in the head, but nobody got really hurt. Since then I keep my eyes open and watch for him every time we go past his landing place.

Five to six miles is a section called Seabreeze with some big hotels and sometimes we stop there and watch the people swimming and playing on the beach. Further down the beach it gets more deserted and one day we saw a big trunk of a tree that was washed up on the beach and left high and dry by the high tide. It was completely covered with what

I first took to be small shells, but as we got closer and inspected it, we could see it was in constant motion and it was covered with some live animals that were growing on the wood. The head was like two-half shells that were opening and closing and they were attached to the wood by a long neck, about one to one and a half inch long and the neck was moving the head from side to side. The neck was fastened to the wood and was of a purple color. The head was white and as the shells opened and closed, it looked like they were sticking their tongues out at us.

I was thinking it was something I had read about that will grow on wooden ships bottom and has to be scraped off every so often, especially when ships are sailing in warm water. No one here knew what it was and I didn't know the English word for it, but in Danish it is called "Langhalse" (Longnecks); if that is what it is.

Halifax river runs parallel with the Ocean, about one mile west and that makes the beach an Island. Everything on the West side of the river is Ormond and on the East side and to the ocean it is Ormond Beach. Further south 5-8 miles is Daytona on the West side of the river and on the East side is Daytona Beach. The river is deep enough to allow pleasure boats to use it and most of the Florida East coast has this river - it is called Indian River farther south. It is mostly salt water as every few miles it is connected with the ocean by outlets, where the tides run salt water in and again out thus creating a strong current in these outlets.

We would sometimes take a trip across a bridge here in front of the hotel to the West side of the river, then go South on a road there till we got to Daytona where we did some shopping. Then across another bridge over the river to Daytona Beach and then back to Ormond Beach, either by road along the river or by way of the beach.

In Daytona there is a steamboat that takes passengers on trips up the river to Tomaka river about 4-5 miles North, then up the Tomaka river where you can see a lot of alligators sunning themselves on the beaches. These are wild, but on some alligator farms we can for a price go in and see them, where they are kept in ponds. Here are a lot of small orange farms where we can stop and pick our own oranges if we want to. Not far from Ormond is a big farm owned by a Swede. He sells oranges for one cent each and he has more than 1000 trees with lots of oranges on them; they are juicy and red. He also has some fruit called grapefruit. That is used a lot in America, but I never remember seeing them in Denmark. They are bigger than oranges and sort of sour, but still good. People eat them for breakfast, it is good for you, and most people put sugar on them.

Then, I see another small orange-like fruit called kumquats. It is a little bitter, about the size of a plum - you eat it skin and all. Oranges and grapefruit are ripe and ready for plucking in December and as late as May, and they need not be picked when they are ripe, they can keep by hanging on the tree all winter until you are ready to use them.

In March, the blossoms come and you often see trees with ripe oranges, blossoms and new fruit on the same tree. They tell me they usually pick the trees clean in April and then dig trenches in the ground where they keep the oranges covered with brush and soil. The oranges will keep better in the cool, moist ground. I bought one box of oranges and grapefruit and sent it to Mrs. Stupplebeen and one box for Mrs. Waltermire. I had a letter from Mr. Stupplebeen yesterday, it had been to Asheville first; I also had a letter from Mr. Waltermire with news from Chatham and thanks for the box of oranges. I hear now Mr. and Mrs. Payn are planning to leave here and go home by the end of next month (March) and I would like to go too, I have not enough here to keep busy and I often go over in the garage and give the car an extra shine just to pass the time.

The hotel here closes in the spring and they move all the help with them to Bretton Woods in the White Mountains in Maine, where they are only open in the summer. It is still cold in Chatham, only ten degrees, and down to zero at times, and here we have a warm winter with 75-80 degrees days and nights down to 55 degrees. It is nice and I wish you were all here, then, I would like to stay.

Love to all

Hal

CHAPTER TEN

Back Home To Chatham

March 4, 1918
On board steamship "Mohawk"

Dear all

As you can see, I am aboard a steamer heading for New York and it was a sudden change in plans. Mr. and Mrs. Payn suddenly made up their minds to go home and Mr. Payn asked me if I thought it would be all right to drive the car back or ship it on a steamer. I think Mr. Hues must have told him about our troubles getting down here, so I told him if it was my car I would ship it, and save the car of the strain it was not really made for, so it was decided to ship the car from Jacksonville and I could go with it. Mr. Payn, Mrs. Payn and

Mr. Hues would go by train, and we all left on Sunday March 3, 1918. It was a short visit to Florida. In Jacksonville the car was put aboard the steamer; it is a passenger Coastal Liner, not very big and it was so full of people that I couldn't get a stateroom or a bed, so I had to sleep in the general public salon on a sofa with about six or eight other men who had no staterooms. Some blankets were hung from the ceiling to sort of divide the room, but I slept good as the weather was good and we are now making a stop of few hours in Charleston.

There were no waves yesterday as the wind was from the West (from the land) and we were sailing along the coast - close enough to see it in the distance. When we sailed from Jacksonville at about 2 p.m. it was warm, about 78 degrees but when I got on deck this morning, it was only 40 degrees and the wind had shifted, so we can expect some rough going when we start from here about 12 noon.

I took a walk in Charleston, had a haircut in a barbershop, and also bought some picture postcards and one cent stamps to put on them to mail them. I have been waiting to hear from Adda now she is married, but now my mail will be interrupted again. With no gasoline in Denmark, I suppose there are no cars running anymore, so I am wondering if I would be able to get a job now and with thousands of people out of work, I better stay here. As soon as I get to Chatham, I am going to try to find out how I stand on being drafted.

We are on our way out of Charleston now and my next letter will be from Chatham. That is all for now.

Love to all

Hal

$50 In My Pocket

March 16, 1918
Chatham, New York

Dear all

I am now writing from Chatham again. I came to New York City Wednesday 11 a.m., and it took some time before the car was unloaded from the steamer "Mohawk" so it was 3 p.m. before I was ready to roll. It was cold in New York and I decided to start for Chatham instead of waiting until the next day, as the weather was clear and there was no snow on the ground. The road was dry and good all the way to Hudson where I arrived at 7 p.m., but from the Hudson to Chatham the road was poor.

At a place near Hudson is a cement plant and near there is a wide creek with a good cement bridge crossing it, and it was closed as it had begun to sink in the ground. It is built on quicksand that has no bottom. They tell me that part of the cement factory sunk down out of sight two years ago. It was the steam power plant with two men inside, I don't know how, but that section suddenly went down; it collapsed, killing the men, and overnight it disappeared in the ground and was never found again.

The building was considered safe, built on iron beams rammed down in the ground, but it was not enough to hold the weight. Now the new cement bridge is going down so they are going to move the road so it doesn't pass over that spot. I had to take another road, but came to Chatham and home that night. I woke up the next morning and there was three inches of snow on the ground and it was cold and freezing down to 15 degrees. It has been a very cold winter here and also many other places. Frith from Bermuda reports a two inch snowfall there, something that never happened before in the known history of the islands. Mr. and Mrs. Payn are not home yet, they are staying in New York and will be up later, I don't know when.

Down in Florida in a garage in St. Augustine I met a Swedish man that drove a car for a millionaire from Delhi in the Catskills, New York State. He had at one time worked in Denmark, about 25 years ago, in a brickyard near our home that was owned by a Mr. Klausen at that time, and he showed me a photograph of him taken in Copenhagen. He said he would see if I could get a job where he was working. These people had this home in Delhi where they stayed four months, then they would go to New York City for two months, then to Florida for four months and then back to New York for two months before returning to Delhi for the summer. I expect to hear from him, but now the first thing to do is to find out how I stand on that draft thing. I miss you all so I just have to get to Denmark again as soon as I can.

Love to you all.

Hal

March 23, 1918
Chatham, New York

Dearest all

I have received a lot of letters - first a letter from Mom sent Jan. 2, then a letter from Dad and one from Solveig. Dad's and Solveig's letter had traveled together here to Chatham March 8, then to Ormond Beach stamped March 11, but that was after I left, then they went to Savannah where Mr. And Mrs. Payn stopped for a couple of days on the way home, but they had left by the time the letters came there, so back to Chatham they went and I got them all stamped and changed addresses all over the envelopes. I also had a letter from my friend Peter, he now works in a machine shop in Copenhagen. I know my sister Adda got married, but I have not heard from her, so please write about the wedding. I am glad you received the picture album from Bermuda. You know I miss Danish pumpernickel, but I can't get it here, still we get plenty to eat and the prices have not gone up too much since the War started for us.

Butter has gone up from 35-40 cents to 50 cents now. A bottle of milk now costs 12 cents, it was 9 cents. Sugar is hard to get and people can only buy two pounds at a time to a family. White wheat flour is also in short supply and you have to buy two pounds of some other kind of flour to get two pounds of wheat; they want to cut the use down to half, so more can go to Europe.

Here is plenty of work for everybody. My friend in Kinderhook, Mr. Ogden, has been in the army since last fall - he was a reserve officer and had to go to France. It seems a shame he had to go over there and some never came back. The snow is now about all gone and the roads are getting dry as we have had a week of warmer weather up in the 60's.

Love to all; tell grandmother I send her a special thought.

Haldor

April 8, 1918
Chatham, New York

Dear all

My friend the Swedish chauffeur from Delhi has sent me a couple of letters asking me to come there and work. He tells me I can get a ten dollar raise from the $70 a month I get from Payn and only the 4 or 5 months they live in Delhi should I supply my own meals, but would have a room. The rest of the year in New York City and in Florida I would get board and room in addition to my wages of $80 and if I wanted to change jobs I could begin there by May 1st.

The trouble for me here is if Mr. Payn goes to Bermuda again next winter. I will be out of a job or will have to go there and get my wages cut to $50 a month as long as we are there. I told Mr. Payn I had been offered a job there and he began talking me into staying here. I would not like to move away from here as I now have a few friends, especially the Stupplebeen's and our neighbors the Waltermire's. Mr. Waltermire has been sick and last winter he was taken to the State Hospital in Poughkeepsie so now Mrs. Waltermire and sister Margaret Kruse and also Mr. and Mrs. Waltermire's daughter, live in that house still waiting for Mr. Waltermire to come back, but I have heard his head is affected and that hospital is a crazy house, so he will never come back.

I still go over to see them in the evenings and play cards with them or just talk telling them about Denmark and now also about my trip to Florida. They just got something new. It is called a Victrola or Gramophone. It cost $85 and looks like a mahogany piece of furniture. It stands on the floor and is about chest high and it is not really uncommon here, but you still see more pianos, as almost every household has one, and some are self-playing. You can play a recording on the Victrola and make it play all kinds of music, or songs almost like the singers were standing right there in the room.

The weather is still nice and warm, up to about 70 deg. in the daytime, but still cold nights.

Love to you all

Hal

April 13, 1918
Chatham, New York

Dear all

Well, I am now staying here for the summer anyway, as Mr. Payn has not yet made up his mind about what to do next winter. If the War ends he may go to Bermuda again and if the War ends I want to go home to Denmark and see you all. The War is dragging out and the American boys are going over there by the millions now, so it is

$50 In My Pocket

not going to last too long. But here is some information about my change of plans. Mr. Payn knew I had been offered a job in Delhi, so the other day I went in his office in the house to talk to him about it and again he tried to talk me out of it. He then asked me how much money they would pay and I told him $80 plus board and room, so I almost fell over backward when he said "if you stay, I will pay you $100 a month and your board and room, so you will be much better off here at least for the summer", and he said that as long as the War was on he would not go to Bermuda, so it looked like I could stay also next winter. That was a good offer and a raise from $70 so I am staying on for a while.

We had nice weather for Easter. Mr. Stupplebeen has left his employment for Mr. Payn and gone to a job in Garden City, Long Island, as caretaker of an estate there, but Mrs. Stupplebeen and daughter Elizabeth are still here as they own the house here on Hudson Ave. corner of Elm. Mr. Payn got another man from Hudson and he has been here all winter now, but is not very good at that kind of work and now he wants more pay. He has been a bartender in New York City some years ago and for the last two days he didn't show up here, so I took care of the heating system in the house (shovel coal in the furnace). So he is finished here. Then, Mr. Payn's coachman, Frank, wanted more money. He is a married man and has been getting $60 a month, when he heard I was making $100 a month, he wanted more money. Mr. Payn refused so he left after working seven years for Mr. Payn. Some things are now getting more expensive so Frank went to Albany and got a job for the post office transporting mail from the trains to the post office, 8 hrs work, one day off a week, and $75 a month to start. He is leaving May 1.

The stable boy also leaves when Frank leaves, he don't want to work here for a new boss, so now it looks like I will be the only one left of the old gang and we will see who comes now and what comes next. Hope Grandmother is over her cold and feels better. I use my motorcycle now that the weather is better.

Love to all

Hal

April 22, 1918
Chatham, New York

Dear all

I just had a card from Soren's sister Marie, she writes that my grandmother died and I am very sad and worried about it. I had so hoped she would be there when I got back. I knew she had been tired for a long time and had that bad cold this winter and now I will be anxiously waiting for your letter. Marie's card got here in one month so that is why I didn't hear it from you as your last letter was from February 19th.

So Soren is now a detective and doesn't have to walk a beat any more. That is good and he now gets 3000 krones a year, that is about $800 a year and that is just a start.

You want to know about the Waltermire's. I can tell you they own the house they live in next to Stupplebeen's and there is Mr. and Mrs. Waltermire, her mother Mrs. Kruse, and her sister Margaret Kruse; then there are two children, Margaret called Honey and Earl, the son. Mr. Waltermire works in the shirt factory where he irons shirts. Mrs. Waltermire and her sister Margaret sew shirts in the factory. Mr. Waltermire gets $ 3.75 per day, eight hours, and the women get $ 3.00 per day. Saturday is 1/2 days work, but they get a full day pay for that, so it is six days pay every week. Mrs. Waltermire's mother is German, but has been here since she was 18, and she says "If I could get my hands on "The Kaiser", I would cut his head off, so that War would end." The little boy Earl doesn't want to be called a German, that makes him mad.

The Red Cross is always trying to get money, they need it for the boys overseas, they give them coffee and doughnuts or cigarettes and now they are asking everyone to donate $1, then you get a little paper red cross to glue up in your window so every passerby can see that you gave. Chatham is suppose to raise $146.00 and they have already now, in ten days reached the $90 mark. Some of that is in bonds you buy and get paid 4 1/2 % from. That money will be paid back to you in ten years, that is 1928. That is all for now, not much news to write about.

Love to all

Hal

May 7, 1918
Chatham, New York

I just got a letter from Mom, it has been 2 1/2 months getting here. I am well and I am hoping you are. The papers here are full of stories about the Spanish Flu spreading all over Europe and people dying like flies. It has even begun to show here. The War must be responsible for that and we hear 10% of the people in Europe now are sick and a lot of them dying. People here are getting very much afraid of it, and there is nothing that can be done about it. In the paper you read there are long lists of people dying or missing in the War too, so this world is getting to be a tough place to live in, but we can't get off and hide anywhere. I can see where prices in Denmark are skyrocketing out of sight. The big Liberty Loan went over the top here and everywhere in the country. Chatham raised $244 that was $100 more than was expected. The last day of the drive for the money, April 26, was declared Liberty day and was a legal holiday and we had parades and speeches. You could buy shares for $50, giving 4 1/2% interest paid out in gold in 1928. If you don't have the money, you can pay $1 a week and the bank will take care of it and give you your bond when it is paid.

On Saturday, the last day of the drive, speakers were in front of the Chatham Bank standing up in the seat of a car talking to the crowd about money to end the war, "to end all wars", about liberty for the world. The last speaker was Mr. Humfred, the cashier from the Bank, and when he told the crowd about the amount of money raised, everybody clapped and hurrahed, then the church bells started ringing and the whistle on the shirt factory also started.

Two men dressed as Uncle Sam rolled a big ball from Buffalo to New York and collected money on the way. The money will end the war soon and bring the boys back home.

May 10, 1918

I have not got this letter mailed yet, so I have just been on a trip to Hudson and the road goes through Ghent, and then it runs past farms with fruit trees all in blossom now. Apple, pear and cherry blossoms everywhere; also the lilacs are now in blossom and it was a pleasant and beautiful trip. Mrs. Payn is now looking for a new cook. Here it is just rich people that can afford and have maids to help in the house, and when I tell them that in Denmark every farmer and a lot of people in the city have maids, it sounds unbelievable to them. A farm wife in Denmark usually has three of four maids and they have to help with the milking. Most all girls, when they are out of school in Denmark, must work as maids to learn to cook and clean. That is considered a necessity before a girl gets married, but I guess the girls here are different.

Mrs. Payn asked me to see if I could get someone from Denmark to come here, so you can look around, they may pay her fare to get here.

The axle on the sidecar of my motorcycle broke the other evening when I was in Valatie and in the dark I hit a boulder in the road. The sidecar dropped down and when I looked back, there was the wheel in the road. I left the sidecar in a shop in Valatie and drove home without it. The letter about Adda's wedding is lost, I am sure, I didn't get it yet. That is all

Love

Hal

May 30, 1918
Chatham, New York

Dear all

Letter from Mom arrived. It was mailed April 4th. I am happy to hear Solveig is doing so well in school. If she wants to she should go to the University and continue her studies, but that is expensive, I know, and I would be glad to help as long as I get $100 a month I can easily save $25 of them every month, I could send that to pay for her books and living expenses, but she may, like Adda, get a boyfriend and get married. The War is going on and on now we have 500.000 men over there and they are still shipped over by the thousands, but we are one year too late, late is better than never, and it is not going to last long now. All factory output is for the War effort, on the roads we see long lines of new trucks loaded with cannons and all kinds of material going to New York to be put on board ships for Europe, and the Allied (our side) are getting stronger every day. We are now told no meat will be sold for two months this summer when we have plenty of vegetables to eat, as all the meat is needed in Europe. I don't care if they do that, in Denmark we never eat as much meat as they do here, so I wouldn't miss it too much.

I send love to you all, Adda, Solveig, Aunt Nora, Uncle Anton, Soren and my dog Pussi - also to you, Dad and Mom.

Hal

Lis Clark

June 28, 1918
Chatham, New York

Well, this year, I got my birthday letter almost two months early, for some reason the letter intended for my Aug. 19 birthday got here in two weeks instead of the usual two months, so thanks for it. I wish I could plan to go home, but that is not possible now for a while.

It looks like the Germans have started to break apart from other partners, Austria and Italy. We have had a nice spring here, but now we have cold and rainy weather and people had to start the furnaces again to keep warm, it even snowed a little the other day, but summer will be here soon, it always does.

There is a shortage of gasoline and it is a rumor. (I hope it is a rumor only) that all private pleasure driving is going to be stopped; but I think Mr. Payn can get gasoline if he wants it. If it comes to be that way, I will look for a job in Detroit until the War is over. When I left Denmark on the ship from Copenhagen, we met a liner coming in from the United States as we passed Elsinore, and I said to myself, it will be a happy day for me and I think also for you, when I will be on a returning ship, I hope it will be soon.

Love to you all

Hal

August 9, 1918
Chatham, New York

Dear all

It is your birthday on Sept. 8 and I think this letter may reach you by then DAD, so I wish you a happy birthday and hope you feel better again. I understand some of my letters have been lost on the way over, but that is to be expected now. I hope you see in the paper how the Allies, now that the American boys are there, have got the Germans on the run. But everyone hopes they will keep up the chase until they are in Berlin, so they can tell the Kaiser "Bill, you are finished, get out, disappear, go out and sweep the sidewalk or something like that." It is going to be a hard time here and over there too, but now it is going the right way and as soon as it is over I will buy a ticket and go home again. It is hard for the farmers here to get any help so they are selling off the cows, and we are now getting more meat and you see a lot of mechanized farm machines and tractors pulling plows; that is a big auto-like machine with iron wheels and they are using them in the fields to pull farm machines; some are pulling as much as four plows or a combine.

People on vacation are now asked to take their vacation working on a farm to help the farmers. More people are sick with the Spanish Flu. It is brought here with the ships it is said.

My motorcycle is giving me a chance to get around when I am not working; I would like to drive over to the New South Berlin to see Mr. Bruen and his wife, Elizabeth. I have had a couple of letters from them. You remember them, she is our dentist's daughter and they are trying to live off a farm out there about 80 or 100 miles from here. If I get a chance, I will go. I will write soon again.

Love

Hal

Aug. 21, 1918
Chatham, New York

Dear all

My birthday on the 19th was just like any other day here, but I have had a trip to New York. You see the other day we were on a short trip to Malden Bridge and the limousine broke an axle. We had to send for the Coachman to come and get Mr. and Mrs.

Payn. Mr. Payn was mad about the car breaking down, he claims the cars are just a passing fad and the horses will again take over. "You can't depend on the damn things", he said. Yesterday, I went to New York to pick up a new axle, but had only a short visit in the big city.

Mrs. Stupplebeen would have liked to go with me and visit her husband who now works someplace on Long Island. He has only been home twice this summer. When it got time to go, she couldn't get anybody to stay in the house and take over, as Mrs. Stupplebeen's mother is not feeling very good and cannot be there alone, so I took Mrs. Kraus, Mrs. Waltermire's sister, with me instead. She wanted to go to Mt. Vernon and visit friends of the Waltermire's, by the name of Winkler, They have a little grocery store there.

So I had company down there and I also know the Winkler's well. We left at 6:30 a.m. and were in Mt. Vernon at 11 a.m., where she got off and I continued to the factory in New York. Mr. Payn wanted me to leave the open car there for some minor repairs and come back on the train; so I left the car there, got the axle and took the train back to Mt. Vernon, where I had a late lunch. Mrs. Winkler wanted me to stay till the next day, but we had to get back on the evening train, so we left and got to Chatham 9 p.m.. Mrs.. Stupplebeen gave me a fountain pen for my birthday. She said she wanted to give it as this was my home here and to consider it as such as long as I am in this country. I got the big car fixed, so now we are rolling again.

Love to all

Hal

**Sept. 8, 1918
Chatham, new York**

Dear all

Today it has rained all day and it is cold enough to stay near the kitchen stove as the big furnace is not started yet. I got a bunch of letters this week - one from Dad, two from Mom, mailed in July, two picture cards and one letter from Adda where she tells about the piano you gave her for a wedding present. That was a big surprise for her, and just what she would like to get.

The Chatham Fair has just ended and I drove Mr. and Mrs. Payn there every day for the horse races. The exhibits are wonderful, especially a lot of motor plows and something you can't believe - milking machines, that is saving labors on the farms. Also a new kind of tractor with a belt-like track on each side instead of wheels. As it goes it puts down a track and picks it up again after going over it, that is really something to see.

Mr. and Mrs. Payn have guests, Mr. and Mrs. Collins and their granddaughter. They are going to New York tomorrow and I am going to drive them there, then leave the limousine, the closed car, at the factory and pick up the other car that has been checked and now is ready to go, so I will drive that back.

This country is now producing so much war material that when we go to Albany we see long columns of trucks going to New York on the main road. It is a new big truck and the wheels are spaced so flanges on the inside of the wheels will fit a railroad track, so these trucks can be driven on a railroad track where no roads are usable. You have to be impressed with all the things you see moving to the ships for use overseas. According to the reports it is also too much for the Germans and they are now falling back. It is not going to last long now, and as soon as it is over, I will be home.

Love Hal

Lis Clark

Sept. 15, 1918
Chatham, New York

Dear all

I long to hear from you, no letter this week, but I know they are on the way and not much going on here. My stomach has been upset and it started in New York when I was there last week. Mr. and Mrs. Payn traveled there on the train and Mr. Collins and family drove down with me. That was last Monday. Wednesday, Mr. and Mrs. Payn went home again after seeing a couple of shows here and a drive in Central Park.

Thursday, the other car was ready to go, they have had it now for 3-4 weeks for repairs and I got that and left the open car here, so I was prepared to leave Thursday morning with Mr. Collins and family, at 8 a.m. I went to bed at 10 p.m., and I slept for about one hour when I woke up sick to my stomach, and I had to rush for the toilet to throw up, and I had cramps most of the night and I never fell asleep again till 4 a.m.. I had asked to be called at 7 a.m., but was not called and it was 8 a.m. when I woke up. I jumped out of bed, got my clothes on and ran for the car. I didn't shave and I couldn't eat anything anyway, as I still didn't feel right, so I got over to Mr. Collins' hotel at 8:20 a.m., and the Collins' were standing on the sidewalk waiting for me. I excused myself and told them why I was late, the first time since coming to this country, and they told me they were starting to worry about me, and they didn't know where I was staying so they had no way to contact me.

The Collins' wanted to go to Hudson, so we got there after a stop in Poughkeepsie for lunch, that is for them - I still couldn't eat. Since coming home, I have had nothing but tea and toast and the first thing I did was take a big dose of castor oil. I feel well now, but I am still not eating very much, I am keeping to tea, oatmeal, eggs and toast.

Mr. Payn told me they were going away for the winter, but not taking the car. They would go to Bermuda, if the war ended; else to Florida by ship, but no car; so I told him I would leave Oct. 1, and try for a job in a factory as they are all advertising for help. The Waltermire's have been in correspondence with the Winkler's in Mt. Vernon - Mr. Winkler now works in the Remington Arms in Bridgeport and his wife is running the store and he is an inspector there. He will get me a job if I want it for the duration of the War.

Henry Ford is now turning out trucks by the thousands and he also is starting to make small, fast destroyers built on a moving track and after the same plan he makes cars. He said "I am not building them, I am fabricating them". He is now finishing one every other day. He has bought a tract of land near Albany, where he intends to build tractors (Green Island), near Troy, and no worker will get less than $5 a day.

Mr. Stupplebeen is also asking me to come to Long Island where he is. I will tell you soon where I will be.

Love

Hal

October 4, 1918
Chatham
Friday afternoon

I have been lazy so it is now about three weeks since I sat down and wrote a letter to you. I am not working for Mr. Payn and I am taking a small vacation after working for two years here including Sundays and holidays. I had two letters from you and one picture card mailed from Svendborg, and it is surely a beautiful city. I have been there once, but it was in the wintertime and it was not very beautiful then, but I must have had a nice vacation there.

Last Monday was my last day on the job and I said good-bye to the cars that I have fiddled with for two years. Mr. Payn got a man from our neighbor city of Ghent to drive the cars and he was here Monday, and I showed him the work he had to do and how to take care of the cars, but actually he is not a professional chauffeur as I soon found out, and he said he had been a barber. He has an old car he goes back home with and he didn't know much about cars, but now it is up to him.

I was to the dentist in Chatham, Dr. Walker; his home is across the street from Stupplebeen's so I know him well and he has a big car, a Hudson Super Six. I was in his office Wednesday and he put two platinum fillings in and one gold crown on yet another tooth, so now I have two gold crowns and I am almost beginning to look like an American. He said to me if you will wash my car this afternoon, I will not charge you the two dollars for the two fillings, just five dollars for the gold crown, so I paid five dollars and washed his car.

He then said he had to show the car to a man that wanted to buy it in Albany Garage and if I could take it up there he would put a gold corner on one of my front teeth that I had knocked a piece out of about 8-10 years ago when I ran into a streetlight stand in Copenhagen.

I did that Thursday - drove it to Albany Garage, showed it and got the man to buy it and then drove it back to Chatham and Dr. Walker fixed my tooth so now I can smile and show a mouth full of gold.

Today I went to Hudson to get my first papers and then I was told I could have had them the first day I was here two years ago, but it makes no difference - I still have to stay here five years to get my citizen's papers.

I wrote a letter to the Remington Arms in Bridgeport, they make rifles and pistols in their plants, and inquired about a job. That is where Mr. Winkler from Mt. Vernon works, and I got a form to fill out from them. I filled it out and mailed it to them, and now after two weeks I have heard nothing from them. They may think I am a German spy or something, so I think I will drive over there or I could go to Ilion, near Syracuse, where there is another plant and that is only 25-30 miles from where the Bruens have their farm.

Yesterday afternoon, Mr. Payn sent for me to come up to see him. Mrs. Payn told me the new man didn't drive the car very good, if I would take him out in the car and give him a lesson in driving it. I did that and now I know he is one of those people that knows it all and he acted like he didn't need any lessons and I later heard he told one of the girls in the house that he was not going to have a foreigner tell him how to drive. Mr. Payn heard that too, and sent for me again and now Mr. Payn said tell him all about it and if he still don't want to learn he will find himself out of a job.

So today, I was out with him again and now he seems willing to learn. Mr. Payn also said if I would come back and drive for them until they left for the South he would send that guy on his way, but I said I would rather try something else now as long as he had someone to drive and it would only be for a short while anyway.

Mr. Payn then said he would keep him on "until we leave, and then when we get back in the spring you can come here again. I will be glad to have you." I told him I would be happy to keep that in mind and if I didn't like factory work I could come back. He then said "You have had some trouble and work here the last couple of days, so this is for you", and he put ten dollars in my hand and also gave me a letter;

Sept. 30, 1918

Payn Ave. Chatham, New York

To whom this may concern

The bearer, Haldor Baarvig, has been in my employ for more than two years as chauffeur, in which capacity he has been outstandingly satisfactory.

He is a careful, experienced driver and I believe him to be honest and sober.

Signed

Louis F. Payn

Next week I plan to drive out to South New Berlin to visit the Bruins and then go to Ilion and see what they have to offer. The other day when I was in Albany, I stopped in at a small machine shop and asked them if I could get a job there. They said I could as a machine operator and they would pay 32 cents an hour the first week while I was being tried out and after that the same as they pay the other men. That was piecework and it depended on my output, but they only had night shifts open, so I said no thanks and left.

I am enclosing a couple of clippings from the "Times Union", our Albany daily paper. One clipping is a picture of Prince Axel of Denmark on a visit to Washington DC, the other is an article about the Spanish flu, it is now a full blown epidemic here, and people are very much afraid of it. It is so serious now the schools are being closed, also theaters and churches - everyplace where people congregate and still it spreads. There is a tale going around that it is caused by a German doctor that worked here in one of the training camps and used the bacteria to inoculate the soldiers so they all got sick; it is probably not true, but it is very bad in the camps and a lot of the young men never get to Europe - they die right here.

Love to you all, Hal

Oct. 10, 1918
Chatham, New York

Dear all

I made the trip to the Bruins and that was a very interesting drive. I got there Monday at 8 p.m., and when I knocked on the door, Elizabeth opened it and she didn't know me at first until I told her who I was. I had changed some since she last saw me about five years ago. I knew her right away and she then asked me in. She had gained a few pounds, but looked good and tanned. After a little while she told me her husband was in the barn across the yard, so we went out there to talk to him, and he knew me right away. He is somewhat deaf, so I had to talk rather loud for him to hear.

After he finished his chores we went back to the house and had something to eat. He had a little mustache, but had not changed much. They could hardly talk English, but talked Danish on the farm and only English when they had to, and they have now been here six years, and I, after 2 1/2 years talk much better English than they do. They talk a broken language, mixing English and Danish, but of course I understand them well enough.

They have an old farm that needs paint badly and the barns look like they could blow down with the first windstorm. The space in front of the door across the yard to the barn was a mess of mud, manure, woodpiles and old farm machines and you really needed rubber boots to walk outdoors. They now have three horses, one young one, one pig, 18 chickens, 12 cows and five calves; 90 acres of land, some in woods and Mr. Bruen milked the cows twice a day. He and his neighbor took turns driving the milk to the Dairy every morning. He can just talk about farming and knows nothing else. He doesn't want to go back to Denmark. The farms there are too expensive, he said he can't get a farm like this for the kind of money he paid for this. Elizabeth wants him to sell and go back to Denmark where he had a good job as bookkeeper in the lumberyard. He said after the war the prices are going to be higher on farms, so if he has to leave he will wait till he can make some money on the place.

They don't have much of any furniture and it is sort of drab and cheap looking. In the kitchen, they have running water that comes out of a pipe connected to a spring up in the field behind the house. Cold water is always running, summer and winter. Elizabeth goes out in the yard 25 times a day to bring in some sticks of wood for the stove and fireplace and her hands are red and rough, not the lady hands she had when she was living home. He gets up about 7 a.m. to feed and milk the cows, then breakfast about 9 a.m. and he is now trying to plow up a piece of land that was used for grass. He would like a Danish boy to help him after the War.

South New Berlin is two miles away and it is a bad kept country road. Gilbertsville is four miles from there. I stayed over night, had a nice breakfast and went to Chatham again. I didn't go to Ilion as I didn't like the country around there. I guess it reminded me of South Carolina.

I am going to Long Island tomorrow and visit Mr. Stupplebeen. I think he has something for me. He is in Hempstead and I am going by train to New York. Then with subways to Hempstead. I can get a job in a garage there and that may be better than Bridgeport as the Spanish flu is spreading through all the factories all over the country. It said in the paper today that Doctors had developed a vaccine for the flu that may help.

The best to you

Hal

CHAPTER ELEVEN

New Job In Connecticut

Oct. 15, 1918
Remington Ave. No. 227
Bridgeport Connecticut

Dear Dad and Mom

I am now here at Remington Ave. in Bridgeport and I had not expected to end up working here. I left Chatham Tuesday and went to Hempstead, where I met Mr. Stupplebeen and we went to the garage he had told me about. They would pay 30¢ an hour, but wanted me to spend about $100.00 for tools I would need, so I didn't take the job yet.

Mr. Stupplebeen took me over to see a big Soldier's Army Camp where the Army collected the men before shipping them to Europe from the

Navy Yard in Brooklyn. There is so much Spanish Flu here so it is unbelievable and we went in a section that was used as a hospital. There were big buildings one after another, barracks full of beds with sick men, at one point we went out a back door and I saw thousands of casket stored there. Just plain pine boxes and Mr. Stupplebeen said the men were brought in the front door sick and dragged out the back door dead, put in a box and shipped home.

I didn't like it around there and was glad to get away from there, so I decided to go to Bridgeport; I am sure it could not be any worse there. I came here this noon as I stayed with Mr. Stupplebeen over night. At 1 p.m. I went to the office of Remington Arms Gun factory and I got a job after showing them the letters I got from them. They had me down for a job as machine adjuster, but gave me a job as clip straightener and I would get paid 42¢ an hour to start. We work from 7 a.m. to 12 noon, and then from 12:30 to 3:30 p.m., that is 8 hours and I could also work 3:30 to 5:30 overtime for 63¢ an hour. Sunday work is double pay. I had to straighten a pistol clip that held the shells so it could work smoothly and easily go into the handle of the pistol. I am making about 5 dollars a day, and I am told there is not much Spanish Flu here yet, and I am happy to hear that, because I and everybody else is afraid of it, too many people die from it.

Love to all.

Hal

Oct. 29, 1918
Bridgeport, Connecticut

I am still here at Remington Ave. where I found a nice room at Mr. Donn's and I am staying here although I am out of work for a few days. I started here Friday a week ago, but I have been trying to contact Mr. Winkler from Mt. Vernon, he is an assistant foreman somewhere in this plant and before coming here it was agreed I would get a job in the same part of the plant he was working, but I have not seen him and I lost his address here, so I had to write to Chatham to get it; so I have been working on the job I first got. I asked in the office if I could get moved to Mr. Winkler's building and was told yes, I could. When I got Mr. Winkler's address and building location in the Plant, I took that to the office and asked to be transferred. Now they moved me to a job I didn't want. I was still listed as a barrel straightener, so they took me to a room like a blacksmith shop and put me to work straightening gun barrels. The barrels would come out of an oven red hot. It was a long barrel for a machine gun and some were bent by the heat. I had a six pound hammer and another man would grab the barrel out of the oven and put them on an anvil and mark them where I should hit them to make them straight. I worked at that and was played out by night, so I told the foreman I couldn't do it, but he said he had no one else and I would have to stay there until my transfer came through.

I again went to the employment office and asked them to move me, and they said if I could wait a few days, there would be a job in Carlton Winkler's department, but I would need an order from my present foreman. They were giving me the run-around and I quit right there, and walked out because my foreman would not let me move, he needed me. This was on Friday, so I contacted Carlton on Saturday and he said he would have a request for me in the employment office on Monday. Monday, I again went to the office and they said as long as I quit, it would take three days to process my new application and to come back then, so now I have a few days off. I went to the factory doctor while waiting and got a shot of serum that is going to keep me from getting the flu, so now I hope I don't get it.

Love to all

Hal

Lis Clark

Nov. 10, 1918
Bridgeport, Connecticut

Today is Sunday and I have time to write letters and I am mailing all my Christmas cards to Denmark. The War is almost over and last week we had fake reports about the end of the War. I was working as usual in Mr. Carlton Winkler's Dept. and about 3 p.m. when the papers came out with a special telling that the war had ended and the Kaiser had signed the peace agreement. The church bells were ringing all over the city and people were hanging out their flags.

Everyone stopped working and collected by the foreman's office and paperboys came running with extras. It was close to quitting time, so we all went home and then we heard the War was still on and it was a false report, but people were going wild in the streets Half the newspapers sold had headlines like "Germany quits", get the latest news, and other newspapers said "Not yet, but soon".

The bells stopped ringing and I went home and to bed. Next morning the War was still on and it was back to work. If the War ends now we will still have to work for some time and the government will need to build up their supply of weapons. I hope it will end soon so I can get home and visit you all, it surely is a long time to be away from home. Mom is asking in her last letter if I have a girlfriend and am thinking about getting engaged. And I can only say, no, there is not even a remote possibility of that.

I was going to mail this in the morning, but the next day, November 11, 1918, the War ended for sure this time. I was in bed sleeping when I heard noise in the street, people shouting. I thought it was late in the evening when I woke up. I took a look at the alarm clock and it was 3 a.m.. I thought it was some people coming home early in the morning and went back to bed. I went to work in the morning, and just as we got ready to start working, the Church bells started ringing again and someone had formed a parade and came marching right through the

$50 In My Pocket

building where I worked. The war is over, they shouted, "The Kaiser is finished".

Everyone joined the parade and we wound through the plant and outside onto the street. Thousands joined in and we marched downtown with flags and horns. Later the papers estimated 50,000 people were in the street. I saw four men carry a wooden box on their shoulders and a sign on it said "This is Kaiser Bill". Others had dummies on stretchers marked "This is the end of Bill". The Kaiser was hung 25 different ways and he was dragged along the street with a rope around his neck. He was hung by his neck from a building and someone had a sigh that read "The Huns are done", another sign said "It was up to us to lick them and we did", another read "We caught the Kaiser with his pants down".

After a while I got tired and went home for dinner and now it is 3 p.m. and I can still hear the noise whistles and church bells go as they have been all day. I hope we can go back to work tomorrow. I wish you all a merry Christmas and a Happy New Year and hope to see you soon.

Love to all

Hal

Nov. 17, 1919
227 Remington Ave

I am still working, but no more overtime. Now that the war is over I am getting my mail directly here. Glad to know I am now an uncle and Adda had a little girl. Congratulations to you two as grandparents. I just picked up my laundry from the Chinese laundry. We have everywhere in this country in most cities, towns or villages a Chinese working for himself and washing and ironing, it seems night and day.,

I don't remember Adda's name very well - Soren's name was Nielsen when I was home, but now it is Waarkjaer, I will write to them soon.

Lis Clark

I am going to inquire about going to Denmark and I heard the price for a ticket now is twice as high as it was when I came here. Then it was $50 now it is $100. And I also saw in the papers that nobody was allowed to go to Europe until things were settled and food again was plentiful and all the American soldiers were transported back home again, so I will stay here for a while until I know more about what is going on.

Love to all

Hal

Nov. 20, 1918
Bridgeport, Connecticut

Dear all

I am thinking about the winter coming now. It is cold out now, we have heat on here in the house. I think if I am still in this country next spring, I will go back to Chatham and work for Mr. Payn again when he comes back to Chatham. Everything here is getting very expensive and some people are moving from here, going home, I think.

Mr. Carlton Winkler is still working here, but I don't see much of him except at work as he goes home to Mt. Vernon every weekend. I finish work every day at 3:30 p.m. and have a long time till bedtime that I don't know how to spend. I sometimes go to a picture show and have an ice-cream soda in the ice-cream parlor before going home, but the time moves slowly and I am wondering if I could get a second job somewhere. I would like that.

Love to you all

Hal

Nov. 24, 1918
Bridgeport

The War is over, but in Europe everything is upset and it is impossible to say when things will settle down. Our President is soon going to travel to Europe to sign the documents officially ending the War and then the boys will be starting to come back. I understand the Kaiser is out and they are going to vote on some of the border locations with Germany, like South Jutland that the Germans took from Denmark in 1864.

Now if the people want to go back and belong to Denmark they can vote on it. In Russia it is now real bad. The Revolution there now is in full bloom. The soldiers are killing all the officers and many other people, everyone with money or a high position or in politics is being killed, but I hope peace will come to all soon.

The censor is not going over my letters any more, so the mail will move much faster, and you and I will get news while it is still news.

People here are feeling the end of the War in their pocketbooks most, a lot of people are losing their jobs and the newspapers are discussing the difficulty of changing the country back to a peaceful living and economy. We have two million soldiers in France and they all want jobs when they get home and it is hoped Europe now can buy everything we can produce. I had a letter from Mrs. Stupplebeen that her mother, that had lived with them most of the time, had died, and I sent a wreath.

More soon

Love to all

Hal

Lis Clark

Nov. 27, 1918

I hear we have enough work here to last until New Years, then they are going to shut down and convert this factory for making something else. It may be automobiles, as they have not been made as long as this war has been on except for the Army. So many thing were not made during the War, but it is going to take time to change over. I am now working everyday and I plan to go to Chatham as soon as work stops here.

I had another letter from Mrs. Stupplebeen asking me to come back if I lose my job here and she also said she saw Mr. Payn's horses go by the house on their way to Hudson and she surmised it was for shipment to New York and then Bermuda.

Beautiful Bermuda, with all the Negroes, Portuguese, white houses, big hotels and flowers, also the mixed money exchange. If I am stuck here for the winter it will be my first winter here. It is cold now, but it is most likely a bit warmer here than in Chatham as the ocean is right on our doorstep. I am now sending this and you may get it before Christmas now that the War is over.

Love to all

Hal

CHAPTER TWELVE

Tragedy Strikes

*1204 Noble Ave.
Bridgeport, Connecticut
Dec. 4, 1918*

*To Mr. L. Baarvig
Slangerup, Denmark*

Dear Sir:

Your son Haldor M. Baarvig is in the Bridgeport Hospital, dangerously ill from Spanish influenza, and I would like to know what you would want me to do with him in case the worst should come. I am in charge of his affairs here and have got the head Doctor interested in Haldor. Dr.

Waterhouse tells me Haldor has a remote chance and he will do all that is possible for mortals to do, but in case the worst comes, I would like to know your wishes.

Your friend

Carlton B. Winkler

Mr. Carlton B. Winkler

$50 In My Pocket

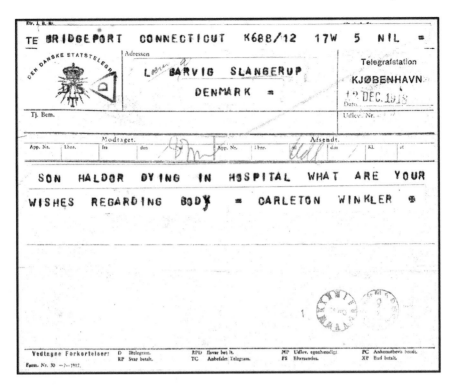

Actual Telegram sent to Hal's Mother and Father

Dec. 19, 1918
Burnham Ward, Bridgeport Hospital

Now you are getting the first letter from me after I was taken sick with the flu, and as you can see, I am still alive. I suppose you got Mr. Carlton Winkler's telegram and he has told me the story of what happened. I am glad I didn't die this time even if I was close to it. Nov. 28 was thanksgiving and a holiday and I didn't feel very good and could not eat any breakfast or lunch, so I went out for a little walk to get some fresh air, but by late afternoon I was really sick and went to bed early.

Next morning, Saturday, I was still sick and stayed in bed and asked Mrs. Donn to send for the Doctor. He came and examined me and said I had the Spanish Flu and high fevers and that Doctor was more interested in his three dollars than to get me well, so he said I should stay in bed and Mrs. Donn could look after me. I don't think she liked that very much as I didn't see her all day except at mealtimes, and I couldn't eat, but I stayed here.

The Doctor must have known I needed more care than Mrs. Donn could give, but he came for his three dollars every day until Wednesday and I got sicker. When he came Wednesday he said I was better and my temperature was lower. That was not so, and I had a nosebleed twice that afternoon, and Mrs. Donn got very concerned and telephoned the Doctor and asked him to have me out in the hospital, but he said it was not necessary. When I left Chatham that fall, Mrs. Stupplebeen told me to come back to her fast if I got sick, but Bridgeport was too far from Chatham, and I had not the time or energy to travel. Later in the afternoon, Mrs. Donn again called the Doctor and asked him again to have me moved to the hospital or at least come over to see me, and he refused to do either, so she said to him she would not take care of me and if he didn't get me moved, she would call the police and have them take care of it and tell them he had refused to do it. He then called the Hospital for an ambulance and they came 9 p.m. for me and I was put in the contagious ward with other Flu patients, and I don't know much of what happened after that, but I was told later that Mrs. Donn sent for Carlton Winkler and he contacted Mr. Stupplebeen on Long Island and they came up to see me, but I didn't know them or remember it.

Mr. Winkler said he got the chief doctor of the hospital interested in my case and asked him to give me all the care I needed. I got more sick and Mr. Stupplebeen came and he and Carlton Winkler took turns watching me. Carlton sent a telegram to you in Denmark when he was told by the doctors that I was dying, and when he got back to his room from the telegraph office, he found a request from the hospital to come there as fast as he could, they didn't expect me to last much longer. My lips were gray when he got there and my face was purple, so he again sent for Mr. Stupplebeen. I was unconscious for two days, but then I started to get better.

Mr. Winkler stayed with me most of the time and when I got so I could talk again he wrote a letter to you and I also had a visit of a minister from a Church that came looking for me after a request to find me that came from the Danish Ambassador in Washington. I will here enclose a copy of the correspondence Mr. Winkler had with you - his first letter to you was mailed on Dec. 4, and you got it about Dec. 12, just before the telegram. Here it is; and it was, I am sure, a shock to you.

1204 Noble Ave
Bridgeport, Connecticut
Dec. 12, 1918

Mr. L. Baarvig

Dear Sir

Since sending you the cable that your son Haldor was dying in the Bridgeport Hospital from Spanish influenza, there has come a change for the better in his condition. Your son was just as sick as a man can possibly be and live, but I am now glad to say that the crisis has passed and he is on the road to recovery.

When he was taken with this disease, the poor fellow had no one to turn to, to help him and he appealed to me. I was struck with pity at his helpless condition and so gave of my time and my intelligence to save his life. It was a hard fight, but I succeeded in enlisting the aid of those high in influence here and your son was given the best of care that a man could have and I am now happy to say that I think that with careful nursing and obedience on his part, your son will eventually recover and be no worse for his suffering. It is likely that your son will soon be strong enough to write to you himself.

Yours very truly

Carlton B. Winkler

Lis Clark

I understand that you got in touch with the "Ministry of Foreign Affairs" in the Danish State Dept. and asked them to investigate. In the meantime you were waiting for news from them. This is a copy of the letter that they sent to you.

Consul of Denmark
Boston, Massachusetts
Dec. 23, 1918

Regarding the condition of Haldor Baarwig:

In reply to the ministry's cablegram of 16. Dec. I beg to state it has taken a little time to get the desired information, having no address of the parties mentioned, and from the fact of there being several hospitals at Bridgeport.

Mr. Baarwig was finally located at the Bridgeport Hospital where he has been, for the past two weeks, dangerously ill from influenza, which sickness he contracted while living in Bridgeport where he was employed on Government work.

He is now reported as being convalescent and expects to be able to leave the hospital in a few days. His parents reside at Slangerup, Denmark. Having come to this country about two and one half years ago; most of the time since then living in Chatham, New York, to which place he intends to return on leaving the Hospital. His address there being Box 341, Chatham, New York.

As requested, a cable message is sent to the ministry this date, as per enclosed press copy.

Very respectfully

The Ministry of Foreign Affairs

Dec. 31, 1918
Chatham, New York

Now I am back in Chatham and I had quite a time in Bridgeport, but Mr. Stupplebeen and Mr. Winkler did all they could to look after me. I hope you now have the Consul's letter so you know I am all right and that you had a nice and happy Christmas. I know all about influenza now and don't ever want to get that again.

In the hospital the windows were open and covered with gauze to let plenty of fresh air in, and they didn't allow anybody out of bed as long as you had a little fever. Do you remember Mr. Snow? He lived here at Stupplebeen's last year and worked at Borden's dairy. He was not in Chatham anymore, but he was taken sick with the flu this fall and as soon as he was better, his mother let him out of bed and he was so weak he got a heart attack and fell on the floor dead. Mrs. Stupplebeen's daughter Elizabeth has had it, and also Waltermire's two children and her sister, Margaret Kruse, but they all got well again. Margaret Kruse told me Mr. Winkler stayed on in Bridgeport until I got better and then went home to Mt. Vernon to take care of his store there. I left the hospital and paid my bill of $100.00 on leaving,

I went back to my room, packed up my things and the next morning I took a train to Chatham and was glad to get here. It seems people here all knew I had been sick. The Waltermire's had telephoned to the hospital several times to find out how I was doing, and when they heard I was dying, they all cried and it seems a lot of other people here didn't expect to see me again. People would look surprised at me and say "I thought you were dead and buried, so what are you doing here". They even had a prayer for me in Church. Margaret showed me a letter from Mr. Winkler where he said he sat by my bed in the hospital and he saw me so near dead, so he was thinking about how fast it can come to all of us, and he discovered how little he was ready to die; he has since thought more about God and it may have made a better human out of him.

He got thinking God had brought me and him together in Bridgeport to teach him a lesson. He sent the telegram to you when the doctors said there was no hope, and he then didn't hear any word from you before the Minister from the Church in Bridgeport found us after a request from the Consul in Boston. He then knew you were informed about my progress.

Mr. and Mrs. Payn are still here - they were going to Bermuda, but at the last minute they found out the usual steamer was not running that route any more and they could only get passage on a small freighter, so now they are going to Florida via New York and steamer to Miami. They are taking two girls (maids) with them, but not the car. Mr. Payn asked me to drive the closed limousine to New York for some repairs. He didn't want his present chauffeur to do it. He doesn't trust him and he would like to have me back again come spring.

He gave me twenty dollars and I drove the car down and came back on the train. I cleared about 12 dollars that day and it was my first job after getting out of the hospital. Send mail to Chatham now and I will soon write again.

Love to all

Hal

PS Mr. Stupplebeen has been here on a short vacation so he went down with me to New York and did some of the driving.

Hal

Jan. 5, 1919
Chatham, New York

Dear All

It is now 1919, and the time certainly flies. I am now just about back to normal again, but I check with the doctor here and he will not let me go to work for a while yet or travel to Denmark. It would be a good time for me to go now as I have no work and can't take any as I intend to go to Denmark, as soon as I am strong enough and the doctor will let me. I would like to have a good long visit with you and then probably come back here again. With all the expenses I have had I still have enough money left to travel to Denmark and back here again, but I hope I don't have to wait too long.

I am drinking a lot of milk and I am almost back to my former weight. The two weeks I now have been here has been good for me. I got some mail from you and Solveig sent a picture of you and her, all three of you and I am happy about getting that. I keep it in my pocket all the time.

Thanks to you Solveig for that and the books and newspapers. I took the newspapers up to the tailor Christiansen, here in Chatham. He was very glad to get them when I was done with them.

Love to all

Hal

>Jan. 16, 1919
>Chatham, New York

Dear all

I am now strong and fat again and the Doctor said I could start work again, but the only thing I have done was that trip to New York with Mr. Payn's car last week. We had about one foot of snow and I had to drive with snow chains on, but had no trouble. Mr. Stupplebeen has been here on a visit and a few days off, and he helped me drive as he was going back to New York anyway. Now the weather is mild and some of the snow is melted.

Last week, two men I knew died from Influenza.; one was the owner of the taxi service. This would be a good time to start a taxi business, but I am going home and am now waiting to hear from Scandinavian American Line. They have a ship leaving soon. The "Hellig Olav" leaves on Feb. 8 and the next one is "United States" on March 1, so I hope to be on one of them.

Later

The mailman brought me a letter from the steamship line and it is quite complicated to travel yet. The price one way has gone up to $125 from the $50 I paid to get here. I have to get a Danish Passport from the Danish Consul in New York and a permit to leave from Washington. I can only bring clothes and my necessary toilet things in my baggage, as everything else has to be shipped as freight and must be examined by the custom service and an export license is needed. No books or films can be shipped except if it is passed by the censor.

I am going to start sending some of my things by Parcel Post as that way it is automatically examined and passed. So, see you soon.

Love

Hal

**February 21, 1919
Chatham, New York**

As you see, I am still here. I have not written any letter to you in more than a month, as I expected to get to Denmark before the letters, but now I have been disappointed and seen the ships leave without me several times. I have paid my ticket, got my passport, but I am still waiting for the permit to leave from Washington. I had to go to Albany and fill out a form with about 100 questions and they even had an investigator sent to Chatham to interview me, so now I think everything is ready, but the next ship is leaving in about one week, March 1, and I have no word about the papers. They said about 600,000 people have asked for permits and Europe is not ready yet to receive them and I am still waiting.

Love to all, Hal

March 1, 1919
Chatham, New York

Dear all

My trunk is packed and I am ready to leave, but the steamer sails today and I am not on it, I am still waiting. I have been offered a job as chauffeur at a place about four miles from Chatham, but I had to turn it down as I am still hoping to be able to go across the Atlantic. I feel well enough to do something and I am tired of just sitting here. The weather is also getting better and I am getting itchy after getting out on the roads again.

I got my first letter from you mailed after Christmas and I don't understand you still think I am sick and now I am wondering if you got the letter from Mr. Winkler and the cable from the Consul in Boston. Now you know I am all right and I may see you soon. I hope I beat this letter and get there first.

Love

Hal

The following words are Haldor's account of his homecoming and not a letter that he wrote to his parents.

Soon after mailing my last letter, the permit came and I was able to leave on a ship that brought me to Denmark on Easter Sunday. We were quickly passed through the customs and I landed on the streets of Copenhagen and no one knew I was coming on that ship.

It is about twenty miles to Slangerup by train and I took a taxi to the train station. When I got there I discovered I had no Danish money and the cabdriver was nice enough to take my American money. When I got in the station to buy a ticket, they would not take my American money so I talked to the station master and he told the conductor to let me go without a ticket and I could pay as soon as I had the money. It turned out he knew my Dad.

They had not received any of my letters or the letters sent by the ministry about my recovery, so they still thought I had died so when I knocked on the door they were all not only surprised but shocked to see me still alive. I cried and so did everyone else and we had a good time doing that. I then found out that Dad had saved all my letters as bad as some of them were. They even showed me the copy of the death notice that appeared in the local paper. That was eerie and I even shivered looking at it. I was so happy to see my family but I remember thinking that I knew that I would go back to America again, should I have the opportunity. I did, but that's another story. Many years later, I translated the letters to English with the help of my daughter, Lis. I hope that someday they will be enjoyed by my grandchildren and also by my grandchildren's grandchildren.

THE END

ADDITIONAL HISTORICAL INFORMATION

Ellis Island Immigrant Wall of Names

Footnote #2
Interesting historical facts about Ellis Island.

Ellis Island is a small island in the New York Harbor that both New York and New Jersey laid claim to. The Island went under many names through the years. It was known as Oyster Island because of the vast oyster beds surrounding the island. It. was also known as Gull Island and Anderson's Island plus a few other names. It served as a pirates nest and then served as a strategic military post to protect the New York Harbor. This was part of a defense system that included several forts on several harbor islands. The Ellis Island fort was called Fort Gibson. Prior to Ellis Island being used as an entry portal, each state was responsible for regulating their individual immigration laws. Originally New York's portal of entry was called Castle Clinton and served from 1855 to 1890 with over 8 million immigrants entering during those years. Most were from northern Europe.

Then, with continuing the massive influx of Europeans, the Federal Government saw the need for some order - out of chaos - and needed a way to check each person that came into the country. Not only that they had funds (that's where the $50.00 comes in) so they would not become wards of the government. Immigrants were checked by doctors to make sure that they had no major health problems. Agencies that were responsible for processing the immigrants were the U.S. Public Health Service and the Bureau of Immigration. The nickname for the Island was "the Island of Tears".

After it was closed to incoming immigrants in about 1924, it was used to detain immigrants who had a problem with their entry papers, war refugees and displaced people. During WW I and World War II enemy aliens and/or sailors were detained. It was also used as a training facility for the U.S. Coast Guard.

In 1965, President Lyndon Johnson declared Ellis Island a part of the Statue of Liberty National Monument. It was opened on a part time basis between the years 1976 and 1984. Then a major restoration project costing over $160 million was started and Ellis Island Immigration Museum was opened in 1990 under the name **The Statue of Liberty- Ellis Island Foundation, Inc.** It houses not only a museum but a large genealogy department where you can locate records of those that entered America through Ellis Island. Families of immigrants can also have their names placed on a wall which stands out in a garden area with a view of the harbor (see picture above).

If you want more information on the history of Ellis Island or you wish to look up your ancestors who may have come through Ellis Island go to the website at www.ellisisland.org.

You will also enjoy a visit to Ellis Island. There is a saying I truly believe and that is "You have to learn from the past to know what you should do for your future:

Footnote #4
More about Louis F. Payn

The ancestry of Louis Frisbie Payn begins in 1638 when Stephen and Rose Paine came to America from England. Samuel Paine was one of their children. Then down the line came a Stephen Paine another Stephen, then Ebenezer Payn (changed the spelling of the name). Ebenezer and his wife Keziah settled in Hinsdale, Massachusetts and had nine children. The eight child, born in 1806, was named Elijah Payn. He taught school, studied law and started a law practice in Chatham and Hudson N. Y. He and his wife Rachel had a son and that was Louis Frisbie Payn born January 27, 1835 in Ghent, N.Y.

Louis was schooled locally and the family moved to Chatham. In 1856, he became a deputy sheriff of Columbia County. Harbor Master, for the Port of New York in the 1860's. He was appointed a United States Marshal for the Southern District of New York State in 1877 by President Grant. His nickname became Marshal and that nickname stayed with him the rest of his life.

Louis F. Payn started out his business ventures by building a paper manufacturing business in Chatham in 1890 called Payn's Mill and then switched his plant to manufacturing box board. He then expanded his ventures into the completely different field of oil development in West Virginia and silver mining in Colorado. He amassed a fortune through his success. During this time, he developed an interest in politics. He was a very active supporter of the Republican Party. He started a local paper in Chatham called the Chatham Republican and became a delegate to both the New York State House and a delegate to the Republican National Convention in 1900, 1904, 1908, 1912 and 1916. He was appointed New York State Insurance Commissioner in 1897 and served until 1900. He never pursued public office but had a great deal of political clout. This clout was evident to Haldor as he drove him around to see his friends and the politicians around the state. His political career was not always smooth and he had many political battles that he fought -to get his selection of candidates elected to office.

In his personal life, he married Margaret Stafford in 1857 and they had one son named Elijah L. Payn who attained the rank of Colonel in the Army. He also had a daughter Marle. His wife, Margaret, died in 1898. Mr. Payn married for the second time on December 24, 1902. to Marion K. Heath of Albany, New York. She was approximately 30 years his junior and reported to have been his secretary. Louis Payn lived in Chatham, N.Y. until he passed away in 1925. His personal relationship with his son Elijah was stormy because of his alleged heavy drinking. A lawsuit filed in New York by Elijah's wife Blanche D. Payn alleges that among charges of abuse, excessive drinking, cruelty and abandonment (He had left her in England without funds.) she wished to have an annulment. Louis F. Payn was dragged into this because Colonel Payn's rebuttal produced a letter signed by his wife that she had accepted the sum of $5,500.00 paid by Louis Payn where she agreed to drop all claims against her husband. These charges were later dismissed. There was another incident where Colonel Payn got into a fight with a man in a theater in New York City because Colonel Payn was annoying the man's wife and Colonel Payn ended up smashing his fist into the gentleman's face breaking his nose. Colonel Payn was taken forcibly from the theater. Colonel Payn was arrested and charged with assault. His heavy drinking played a part in this charge.

His passion was his horses. He had both race horses and he had smart looking horses he used to pull his buggy around the village. The village of Chatham was his home throughout his life. He had a deep pride in this community, that he loved .

The Hon. Louis Payn was a force in Republican politics until the time of his death. He passed away March 20, 1923 in Chatham, N. Y., after a bout of pneumonia. He is buried in Chatham Rural Cemetery. Louis F. Payn was a philanthropist who wanted to give back to his community and therefore set up the Louis Payn Foundation, Inc. This Foundation, through the directors, oversees the running of a home for the aged that is a beautiful and safe haven for some of the older residents of the local community.

Footnote #7
More about the Owen-Magnetic Automobile

The Owen-Magnetic automobile was a very unique car for the time it was built. You might say that the engineers were way ahead of their time. This auto is considered a forerunner of the hybrids of today. It was manufactured by R.M.Owen & Co. of New York then Cleveland and finally Pennsylvania. There were several other names and companies involved in its short life. It was built from about 1915 to1921 or 1922. World War 1's need for war goods interrupted the manufacturing of the auto. After the war ended, there were several attempts to start manufacturing it again but nobody seemed to be able to get production going. Approximately 250 autos were produced. It was a very expensive car for that time, costing anywhere from $3,000.00 to $6,000.00. Owen-Magnetics were advertised as "The car of a Thousand Speeds" You can read more and see more pictures of the auto by going to Google and asking for Owen-Magnetic automobile. One sight is Wikipedia, and also - www.JayLenoGarage.com.

ABOUT THE AUTHORS

The writer of all the letters, Haldor Marius Ingemann Baarvig (Hal), was born August 19, 1892 in Slangerup, Denmark. He was the son of Lauritz and Marie Baarvig. Haldor's father was a school teacher in the small town of Kvinderup. He was a good student but very restless. Having been born with a curious mind, his wish was to see the world starting with America. His father was not happy about his wish to go to America as he wanted him to go to Germany to study Engineering. Despite his father's objections, he sailed on June 2, 1916 for New York to start his adventure. He had never been more than 50 miles from his home prior to this undertaking so he was naturally a little bit apprehensive. He was a prolific letter writer and wrote diligently to his family. He wanted them to be able to live his adventure through these letters. He was well aware that they would not be able to come to America. All of the letters were written in Danish. His mother and father kept every letter that was sent to them. Lis Clark is the author who encouraged Hal to translate them into English. This he did, after he retired. More years passed and finally they are in the form that you are seeing and reading today. I have added some additional historical information that I hope you find interesting.

ACKNOWLEDGEMENTS

I would like to thank my daughter Deborah Waarkjaer. Her help was invaluable in typing up the first draft on the typewriter. It was a tedious job trying to decipher the translated transcript. I, also, wish to thank my cousin Helle (I call her my second daughter) for helping me to type it again, into the computer. I wish to thank my good friend Janet Hall for all her help in proofing the manuscript. I, also, wish to thank The Statue of Liberty-Ellis Island Foundation, Inc. and particularly Elizabeth Oravatz for her help in researching some information and also for getting the necessary permission to use some of the photographs that are used. I also, want to thank my husband Edwin for all his patience. He has been listening to me, over the years, how much I wanted to finish compiling this book. Life and excuses kept getting in the way but finally I made the time to complete it. I do hope you have enjoyed reading it.

I would love to hear from the readers. Your comments, good or bad will be welcomed. You can reach me at the e-mail address below:

Lis (Baarvig) Clark

50.dollarsinmypocket@earthlink.net
fiftydollarsinmypocket@yahoo.com

Watch for upcoming website
www.50dollarsinmypocket.com

LaVergne, TN USA
06 April 2010
178402LV00004BA/7/P